James McConica

Erasmus

Oxford   New York

OXFORD UNIVERSITY PRESS

Oxford University Press, Walton Street, Oxford OX2 6DP

Oxford New York Toronto
Delhi Bombay Calcutta Madras Karachi
Petaling Jaya Singapore Hong Kong Tokyo
Nairobi Dar es Salaam Cape Town
Melbourne Auckland

and associated companies in
Berlin Ibadan

Oxford is a trade mark of Oxford University Press

© James McConica 1991

First published 1991 as an Oxford University Press paperback
Reprinted 1991

British Library Cataloguing in Publication Data

McConica, James
Erasmus.—(Past Masters)
1. Scholarship. Erasmus, Desiderius. d.1536
I. Title II. Series
001.2092
ISBN 0–19–287599–X

Library of Congress Cataloging in Publication Data

McConica, James
Erasmus / James McConica.
p. cm. — (Past masters)
Includes bibliographical references and index.
1. Erasmus. Desiderius. d.1536—Criticism and interpretation.
2. Humanists—Netherlands—Intellectual life. 3. Reformation—
Netherlands. I. Title. II. Series.
199'.492—dc20 PA8518.M39 1991 90–42497
ISBN 0–19–287599–X

Typeset by Colset Private Ltd.
Printed in Great Britain by
The Guernsey Press Co. Ltd.
Guernsey, Channel Islands

Past Masters

General Editor Keith Thomas

Erasmus

James McConica is a Fellow of All Souls College, Oxford.
His previous books include *English Humanists and
Reformation Politics* and ... University,
volume 3 of the His...

This book is due for return on or before the last date shown below

Past Masters

AQUINAS Anthony Kenny
ARISTOTLE Jonathan Barnes
ARNOLD Stefan Collini
AUGUSTINE Henry Chadwick
BACH Denis Arnold
FRANCIS BACON Anthony Quinton
BAYLE Elisabeth Labrousse
BENTHAM John Dinwiddy
BERGSON Leszek Kolakowski
BERKELEY J. O. Urmson
THE BUDDHA Michael Carrithers
BURKE C. B. Macpherson
CARLYLE A. L. Le Quesne
CERVANTES P. E. Russell
CHAUCER George Kane
CLAUSEWITZ Michael Howard
COBBETT Raymond Williams
COLERIDGE Richard Holmes
CONFUCIUS Raymond Dawson
DANTE George Holmes
DARWIN Jonathan Howard
DESCARTES Tom Sorell
DIDEROT Peter France
GEORGE ELIOT Rosemary Ashton
ENGELS Terrell Carver
ERASMUS James McConica
FREUD Anthony Storr
GALILEO Stillman Drake
GIBBON J. W. Burrow
GOETHE T. J. Reed
HEGEL Peter Singer
HOBBES Richard Tuck
HOMER Jasper Griffin
HUME A. J. Ayer
JESUS Humphrey Carpenter

KANT Roger Scruton
KIERKEGAARD Patrick Gardiner
LAMARCK L. J. Jordanova
LEIBNIZ G. MacDonald Ross
LOCKE John Dunn
MACHIAVELLI Quentin Skinner
MALTHUS Donald Winch
MARX Peter Singer
MENDEL Vitezslav Orel
MILL William Thomas
MONTAIGNE Peter Burke
MONTESQUIEU Judith N. Shklar
THOMAS MORE Anthony Kenny
WILLIAM MORRIS Peter Stansky
MUHAMMAD Michael Cook
NEWMAN Owen Chadwick
PAINE Mark Philp
PASCAL Alban Krailsheimer
PAUL E. P. Sanders
PETRARCH Nicholas Mann
PLATO R. M. Hare
PROUST Derwent May
RUSKIN George P. Landow
SCHILLER T. J. Reed
SCHOPENHAUER Christopher Janaway
SHAKESPEARE Germaine Greer
ADAM SMITH D. D. Raphael
SPINOZA Roger Scruton
TOLSTOY Henry Gifford
VICO Peter Burke
VIRGIL Jasper Griffin
WITTGENSTEIN A. C. Grayling
WYCLIF Anthony Kenny

Forthcoming

JOSEPH BUTLER R. G. Frey
COPERNICUS Owen Gingerich
DURKHEIM Frank Parkin
GODWIN Alan Ryan
JOHNSON Pat Rogers
JUNG Anthony Stevens
LINNAEUS W. T. Stearn
NEWTON P. M. Rattansi

ROUSSEAU Robert Wokler
RUSSELL Anthony Grayling
SOCRATES Bernard Williams
TOCQUEVILLE Larry Siedentop
MARY WOLLSTONECRAFT William St Clair

and others

Contents

Note on abbreviations

The following abbreviations are used in references given in the text:

A	*Antibarbari*, *Collected Works of Erasmus* (CWE), vol. 23
Ad	*Adagia*, CWE, vol. 31
Ax	*Axiomata*, in *Christian Humanism*, ed. Olin
Bo	Boyle, *Erasmus on Language and Method in Theology*
C	*Colloquies*, ed. Thompson
E	*Enchiridion*, CWE, vol. 66
I	*Institutio principis Christiani*, CWE, vol. 27
M	*Praise of Folly*, CWE, vol. 27
Mc	McConica, 'Erasmus and the Grammar of Consent', in *Scrinium Erasmianum*, ed. Coppens
P	*Paraclesis*, in *Christian Humanism*, ed. Olin
Ph	Phillips, *The 'Adages' of Erasmus*
Q	*Querela pacis*, CWE, vol. 27
R	Rummel, *Erasmus' Annotations*
Ru	Rupp, *The Righteousness of God*
S	*De ratione studii*, CWE, vol. 24
V	Letter to Volz, CWE, vol. 66
W 1, W 2, W 3, etc	Volumes of the correspondence series within the *Collected Works of Erasmus*.

Full bibliographical details of these and other works are given in the suggestions for further reading at the end of the book.

Introduction

Erasmus is the Reformation's orphan. Illegitimate at birth and deprived of his parents as a boy, his origins seem in retrospect oddly prophetic of his role in history. He was passionately concerned to promote the faith and enlightenment of Christendom, but quite unable to give unqualified assent to any of the rival orthodoxies which the civil war among Christians had spawned. Before the time of Luther, he was the most widely read and persuasive critic of the Church which he wanted—like Luther—to reform, but Luther found him equivocal and faint-hearted. To the end of his life he was as stubbornly loyal to Catholic unity as he was independent of conventional ecclesiastical authority, yet he suffered the posthumous excommunication of having all of his works placed on the Index of prohibited books. He lived away from his native Holland and found his most lasting domicile with the Froben press in Basle, but his true homeland was the one he constructed with his pen, through his vast correspondence, his tireless publication—works of devotion, the sources of Christian faith, educational texts and treatises, coruscating satire and social commentary—and withal, through the alluring warmth of his intimate, lucid, and insinuating style. In the centuries that followed, it is not surprising that the defenders of confessional religion have been slow to claim him as their own, nor that his general reputation has been that of the dauntingly witty, erudite, and corrosive critic of official belief and popular devotion. For his irenic and rational faith, however, he has received the unwavering esteem of such as Lucius Cary, Viscount Falkland, who regarded him as one 'who thought himself no Martyr, yet one who may passe for a Confessor, having suffered, and long, by the Bigotts of both Parties'.

In our sceptical and self-consciously tolerant age, Erasmus seems at times to be coming into his own. Until quite recently, the modern revival of Erasmus and his legacy has rested chiefly on the great critical edition of his correspondence by Percy

Stafford Allen, who from 1924 to 1933 was President, appropriately enough, of the outstanding Erasmian foundation at Oxford, Corpus Christi College. The appearance of a comprehensive edition of Erasmus' letters naturally drew the interest of historians to this new window on the Reformation, to concentrate their attention, not so much on Erasmus' vast legacy of scholarship preserved in the Leiden folios of 1703–6 as on this more accessible material, the most important single archive for the intellectual history of the time. But the letters, which were often written or revised expressly for publication, inevitably throw into relief the Erasmus of the public forum, responding to criticism, moving to the attack, adapting to change, pursuing patrons, and justifying his work. Seen through the eyes of the first scholars to exploit Allen's researches in detail, what emerged was the face of the cultivated religious *politique*, the founder of the 'third Church' of Augustin Renaudet, a prophet of the Enlightenment who led his followers 'au doute discret, à une sorte de scepticisme de bonne compagnie, et qui se trahit par le sourire ou par les silences respectueux'. The cloistered smile, the discreet silence, the artful ambiguity, the irreverent wit—these traits still dominate the received view of Erasmus in most classrooms and lecture halls, so that, even among the scholars of today, echoes of the old hostilities can be heard from those who feel that the history of the Reformation really belongs to the confident dogmatists, and that Erasmus, for all of his erudition (or even because of it?) was not, somehow, really serious about religion.

In recent years, however, this appreciation has begun to develop a new dimension. The reasons for this are many, but all derive from a growing interest in the things about which Erasmus was expert—the sources of the Christian faith, the theory and practice of education, the uses of language, the arts of persuasion and satire, the need for social harmony, and concern with the official ideals of our society contrasted against the behaviour not only of those in power, but of the populace who support them.

Within the Christian faith itself, the ecumenical urge to draw together in the face of a diffident world has worked finally to the advantage of the one commanding moderate of the Reformation who refused to fall silent, or to surrender his convictions in the face of warring orthodoxies. The reform programme which he saw founder in his own day has won new attention from those who would like to reappraise the causes of that signal catastrophe in the history of western Christendom. To others, Christian or not, Erasmus' cosmopolitanism and irenicism, his hatred of war and violence, and his championing of international order recommend him equally as a figure for our time. And for those responsible for education in school or university, who lament the loss of a humanism effective in disposing the young to moral and intellectual discipline in the service of the common good, he remains a figure as challenging as he is remote.

The history of Erasmus' reputation should not deceive us into thinking that his influence lay dormant until the Second Vatican Council. In the realm of biblical scholarship, in the theory and practice of education, the articles of devotion, the sharpening of critical attitudes, the propagation of moral wisdom—in all of these spheres his largely unacknowledged presence has been so pervasive that even a century after his death, it became impossible to record.

In this book I have tried to present in brief compass the leading ideas and concerns that explain the importance of Erasmus for our moral and intellectual culture. I have begun with an account of his own formation, which explains not only why his approach to the crucial issues of his day was so unlike that of many of his contemporaries, but also so radically unlike anything to be found in our time. Paradoxically, it also explains why his influence has persisted, flowing quietly around the confessional fortresses to nourish the broad streams that bore the European mind and spirit into the age we call modern. I have dealt with his personal history only in passing, since it was his pen that made him important, and I have concentrated on a few texts, readily available, in which an epitome of his enterprise can be discovered.

1 The making of the grammarian

Erasmus was born in Rotterdam during the night of 27/28 October, some time in the latter years of the decade 1460–70. Our uncertainty over the exact year (1467 is now rather favoured) deserves to be reported, since it indicates at the very outset how little precise information survives about his origins. That this is so is chiefly his own doing. He was regularly inconsistent in reporting his age, and the fullest account we have of his early life, the *Compendium vitae*, is of disputed authorship and certainly tendentious. Tendentious too are the shorter versions he wrote to the authorities, Julius II and Leo X, in order to gain the dispensations he needed to earn his own living while still in religious vows.

His father's family seems to have originated near Gouda, and there is enough casual evidence in the correspondence to support the indications in the *Compendium vitae*, that both his parents' families were reasonably substantial, if not precisely wealthy, people. His parents were unmarried, a circumstance that left him with a relatively routine canonical impediment to ordination to the priesthood. It had also, and for the same reason, to be mentioned by him whenever he sought a dispensation for exemption from any of the obligations of his religious vows, leaving some modern historians with the groundless impression that Erasmus was haunted by his illegitimacy. He had a brother, Pieter, three years his elder; his mother was a widow, and his father at some stage became a priest. The father was himself an educated man who earned his living as a scribe, lettered in humanistic Latin and Greek. Erasmus owned books from his library, and Greek manuscripts copied by him in Italy. Just why the parents did not marry is not clear. The most reliable information is contained in the Brief of Leo X, dated 26 January 1517, which was a private document meant to be kept secret and confidential, and to be used by Erasmus only if the propriety of his clerical status was questioned. It is clear from this, not that his father was a priest at the time of Erasmus' birth, but that

4

there was a canonical impediment to the marriage of his parents, owing perhaps to consanguinity or affinity in a collateral line. If so, it would have required the consent and co-operation of both families to obtain the needed dispensation. The argument of the *Compendium vitae*, that the father's numerous brothers were determined that the youngest of them enter the priesthood, suggests at least one reason why such co-operation was perhaps not forthcoming. At any rate, it is difficult to believe that in this secret document, the Brief of Leo X, intended to serve Erasmus as a last line of defence if his clerical credentials were challenged, we have anything other than an exact remedy for the awkward difficulties surrounding his birth. Otherwise, we must suppose that in a matter of the most vital importance to his personal welfare, he deliberately deceived the highest authority in the Church in order to obtain a document which, used as intended, would have been worthless and even damaging if the account of his birth that it contained were contrary to common knowledge. We know, moreover, that contact between Erasmus and his relatives continued through his later life. The *Compendium vitae*, at least, mentions his having seen two of his mother's brothers at Dordrecht when they were nearly ninety; on another occasion, an unidentified kinsman visited Johann Froben at Basle in 1515 while Erasmus was absent, prompting Beatus Rhenanus to remark to him in a letter, 'the resemblance in feature at once proclaims him a relative of yours'. There is a reference to a paternal uncle Theobald in a letter from Brussels in 1498, and Erasmus was clearly in touch with his brother Pieter until the latter's death in 1527. Such people would have known the truth about the father.

With the death of their parents about 1484, the two boys were placed under the protection of three guardians, one of whom was Pieter Winckel, who had also been Erasmus' first teacher. He taught in the school attached to the church of St John at Gouda. Although Winckel's competence both as a guardian of their inheritance and as a teacher is questioned in Erasmus' various recollections, he is known to have transcribed a manuscript of Juvenal at Louvain, and may be credited reasonably with having helped to lay the foundation for what was to become one of the most prodigious scholarly accomplishments

5

in the history of learning. The two brothers were then sent (about 1478) for further schooling at the famous school of the chapter at St Lebuin in Deventer. The school was not run by the Brethren of the Common Life, as is often asserted, nor was the running of schools the work of the Brethren. Typically, they ran hostels for boarders and poor pupils, and such was the case at Deventer. One of their number, a Jan Synthen, did teach in the school and taught Erasmus, possibly along with the better-known Alexander Hegius. Hegius was a friend of the famous humanist Rudolph Agricola, and by 1483 he had become head-master of St Lebuin's school. If Hegius did not arrive at Deventer until then, he could not have taught Erasmus for more than a year, since Erasmus appears to have left the school and Deventer when the plague struck in 1484. Later, in his *Spongia*, he remarked that he owed little to Hegius, but he spoke of him always with praise. Certainly under the influence of Hegius the Deventer school rose to prominence as a centre of humanistic education, and it seems likely that the school was already well along the road to distinction before Hegius's arrival. At the time of his death in 1498, the school was attended by more than two thousand pupils, and had become a nursery for a generation of Dutch humanists.

About the humanists and their interests a preliminary word must be said. Their bent was opposed to that of the established intellectual culture of the medieval university—of the 'Schools'. In particular they rejected any emphasis upon logic and speculative sciences like metaphysics, in favour of the prac-tical arts of life in society—of persuasion (rhetoric), and its ancillary disciplines like politics, history, and poetry—although they shared an interest in dialectic, the art of argu-ment. More broadly, it may be said that the humanists were absorbed with the place and potentialities of the human indi-vidual in this world, without excluding the perspective of an eternal destiny. These preoccupations reflected the needs of an increasingly urban and literate, lay society first in Italy, then in northern Europe. In classical antiquity they felt they found a distant but seemingly recognizable culture contrasting with that prevailing about them, and having a particular authority for solution of the questions they faced. It became urgent therefore to study the texts bequeathed by that culture, to master the languages which would give immediate access to them, to adopt the stylistic training and standards which produced them, and to take from them the lessons of man's humanity, *humanitas*. This concept implied relation to the community, the exercise of effective freedom of the will, and the obligation as a citizen of a particular town or state, there to serve the common good. The texts of the *litterae humaniores*, of humane letters, of *bonae litterae*— these provided a schooling, therefore, in civic virtue. It must be stressed in our time that this 'humanism' did not imply hostility to or rejection of traditional religion; indeed, it could and did at times form a powerful synthesis with it. In the developing philosophy of Erasmus we shall see all of this demonstrated in magisterial form.

With his mother a victim of the plague in 1483, and his father's death shortly thereafter, Erasmus was sent with his brother to the school at Bois-le-Duc or 's-Hertogenbosch, where once again they stayed in a hostel run by the Brethren. This was a crucial period for the young men, since (in Erasmus' admittedly highly coloured account) Winckel and the guardians pressed them to enter religious life as a solution to their orphaned poverty, while Erasmus at least was keen to go to university. His later account is bitter indeed. Of the Brethren: 'Their chief purpose, if they see a boy whose intelligence is better bred and more active than ordinary, as able and gifted boys often are, is to break their spirit and depress them with corporal punishments, threats, and recriminations, and various other devices—taming him, they call it— until they make him fit for the monastic life. On this ground they are pretty popular with the Dominicans and Franciscans, who say their Orders would soon come to an end if it was not for the young entry bred up by the Brothers, for it is out of their yards that they pick their recruits.' Then, addressing the substance of their teaching, he continues: 'Personally, I believe that even among them there are some quite worthy people, but suffering as they do from a lack of the best authors, and living by customs and rites of their own in a darkness of their own making . . . I do not see how they can give the young a liberal education. Experience shows, at any rate, that no places produce young men more coarsely educated or more depraved in character.'

7

These quotations are taken from a disguised biographical account written in 1516, and known as the 'Letter to Grunnius' (W 4.11). It was published in the *Opus epistolarum* in 1529, and was composed to support his appeal for a further dispensation from his monastic commitments (the first having been granted by Julius II in 1506). It was part of a campaign agreed upon in London with Andrea Ammonio, the subcollector of papal taxes, who was one of Erasmus' closest friends. The campaign was successful, and brought as its trophy the dispensation of 1517 from Leo X. It is important to understand that essential to the canonical case Erasmus wished to make was the contention that he had not entered monastic life with mature judgement and of his own free will, but under age, and only in response to the relentless pressure of his guardians, intensified by his wish to escape from an intolerable situation, including the way of life of the Brethren at 's-Hertogenbosch.

Whatever the exact truth of the matter, after two more years at 's-Hertogenbosch Erasmus' older brother Pieter entered the house of the Augustinian canons at Sion, near Delft, and, a little later, Erasmus joined the same order at Steyn, a few miles away. This was in 1487, seemingly, and Erasmus was about twenty years old (not sixteen, as he would later claim). His only extant letter to his brother is from this time. It is affectionate and cordial, and speaks warmly of a friend in the monastery, Servatius, with whom Erasmus formed a close attachment. To a casual reader the most striking thing about this letter and others of the period is the evidence of familiarity with the style and conventions of classical rhetoric, and of pleasure in the exercise of the epistolary arts. Moreover, Erasmus asks his brother to lend Servatius his small copy of Juvenal's satires, one suggestion among many that the Augustinian cloisters were not entirely inhospitable to humanistic learning. Erasmus' exchanges with Servatius Roger and other of his early correspondents from this time—Franciscus Theodoricus, Cornelis Gerard, and Willem Hermans in particular—all show that the same enthusiasms for the study of good letters were widely shared, while it is also clear that Erasmus was the dominant member of this growing literary sodality. It was the first of many occasions in which he would become the focus and inspiration of a whole literary circle.

Beyond this broad framework of events and our general knowledge of the religious milieu in which he now lived, we have little detailed or clearly unprejudiced information about the early formation of Erasmus, either in the monastery or earlier in his schooling. To say that this formation was humanistic is so general as to be misleading. The details we need we find instead in his own treatises on education, and in his first important work, the *Antibarbari*—'Against the Barbarians'.

The *Antibarbari* is effectively the manifesto of the young Erasmus. It is also an impassioned defence of the study of the classics, and so provides an ideal access to his preoccupations and personal culture. It was begun, as he tells us, before he was twenty, which is to say at about the time he entered the monastery. It had a remarkable history, and like many of his major works, was revised and developed over some years. It was originally conceived in four books, of which only the first survives. This was recovered by Erasmus while he was in Louvain after the entire manuscript disappeared from the custody of friends in Italy, then revised once more and published by Froben in 1520. Erasmus explained that he had found the manuscript circulating unofficially (as was to happen sometimes also to his letters), and to protect his reputation from the juvenile mistakes these versions contained, he produced an official edition. Margaret Mann Phillips, in her English version, has pointed out that in 1520, the *Antibarbari* also contained unmistakable allusions to some of his detractors in Louvain.

The work was originally conceived as a rhetorical speech in defence of the classics, and it retains essentially that form, although the first recasting imposed on it some of the form of a dialogue. The principal speaker is Jacob Batt of Bergen op Zoom, a faithful friend whom Erasmus met shortly after ordination to the priesthood on 25 April 1492, while he was in the service of Hendrick van Bergen, bishop of Cambrai. It was in the bishop's country house at Halsteren, near Bergen, that Erasmus revised the *Antibarbari*, and in the bishop's gardens he created the neo-classical setting for the meeting of friends which opens the piece.

Batt, a graduate of the University of Paris, had been back

9

about two years, having been appointed rector of the municipal school. He then became town secretary, not long before the dialogue begins, which permits a fairly precise dating for Erasmus' reworking of the original speech, between the spring and autumn of 1495. Further additions, including the allusions to theologians and religious orders at Louvain, were added in 1520.

In the *Antibarbari* we seem to have a résumé of Erasmus' personal philosophy, based on the experiences of his youth and early manhood. By the time it was sent to Froben for printing he was in his early fifties, and he had suddenly become at once famous and notorious with the appearance between 1515 and 1517 of two new editions of the *Adagia*, and, above all, the publication of the Greek New Testament, the *Novum Instrumentum*, in February 1516. While its principal theme is a defence of classical learning against the attacks of Christian fundamentalists, the *Antibarbari* moves toward an understanding of the Christian mission which informs all of Erasmus' writing. We are also able to identify the masters from whom Erasmus derived his own inspiration, and to locate him precisely in the history of Christian thought.

In the dialogue, Erasmus plays the part simply of host and (as events prove) recorder of discussion. Batt, cast in the role of the defender of pagan learning, begins with an impassioned account of the difficulties he had encountered as a schoolmaster in trying to improve the curriculum of his school. He is soon given a serious challenge by the burgomaster, in the role of the devil's advocate: Batt's programme implies ('let us be frank') the introduction of heathen authors who are not only difficult to get to know, but who write licentious, even obscene works. 'Now admit the facts: you are rejecting Christian writers and bringing in heathen ones . . . you are forbidding the young to read chaste authors and offering them lascivious ones.' (A 38)

Batt's first line of defence is to plead for genuine knowledge of the pagan authors before judgements are made, since, after all, the entire legacy of our learning comes from those sources. 'If we are to be forbidden to use the inventions of the pagan world, what shall we have left I ask you, in the fields, in the towns, in churches and houses and workshops, at home, at war, in private and in public? To such an extent is it true that we Christians have nothing we have not inherited from the pagans. The fact that we write in Latin, speak it in one way or another, comes to us from the pagans; they discovered writing, they invented the use of speech.' (A 57) He insists on the excellence and virtue of many pagan authors, as he does on the frailty and error of many Christians. 'The books of Origen, censured as heretical in many passages, are read by the Christian church with profit to scholarship; and yet we shun the divine writings of men on whose moral character we cannot pass judgement without the greatest impertinence.' (A 58) It is true that some of the inventions of the pagans are doubtful and unwholesome, but others are useful, health-giving, and even necessary. Why should we not take over the good for ourselves?

From this Batt moves to a more profound reflection: the achievements of the pagans were a part of the divine plan. 'When I look a little more closely at the wonderful arrangement, the harmony as they call it, of things, it always seems to me that it was not without divine guidance that the business of discovering systems of knowledge was given to the pagans.' God, after all, is Wisdom itself, 'establishes all things with consummate skill, differentiates them with beautiful play of interchange, and orders them with perfect rightness'. It was he who willed that the Son, the incarnate Word, should be born in an age which was sovereign over all epochs before or after, and it pleased him that whatever existed in nature should be put to use for increasing the happiness and glory of that time. It was his own promise: 'I, if I be lifted up from the earth, will draw all unto me.' Why did all this happen, if not to ensure that the best religion should be adorned and supported by the finest studies? (A 59)

At this point we find stated the central theme of the book, and indeed the ground of the whole of Erasmus' enterprise: 'Everything in the pagan world that was valiantly done, brilliantly said, ingeniously thought, diligently transmitted, had been prepared by Christ for his society.' (A 60) Later on he adds, 'None of the liberal disciplines is Christian, because they neither treat of Christ nor were invented by Christians; but they all concern Christ.' (A 90) While Christ revealed in his own time the highest good, 'he gave the centuries immediately preceding a

11

privilege of their own: they were to reach the thing nearest to the highest good, that is, the summit of learning'. On this point, God also considered the predicament of the Christians, 'who were likely to have much to do elsewhere' (A 61). Batt goes further: Christians have added nothing to the pagan legacy of learning; more typically, they have brought damage and confusion to the legacy. Batt is not speaking of the mysteries of religion, but of systems of learning. He is adamant: 'In my opinion there is no erudition in existence except what is secular (this is their name for the learning of the ancients) or at least founded on and informed by secular literature.' (A 62)

We are here on the familiar territory of an ancient debate, as Erasmus was well aware. Of particular importance is his invocation of the *preparatio evangelica*—the evangelical preparation of the ancient world to be the cultural cradle of the Christian mystery. In this view, there is less of a gap than one might think between the state of humanity before and after Christ. Man's aptitude for virtue and wholeness existed in part before, not only in pious Israelites, but also in the pagan sages. Their excellence was possible because the grace which abounds since Christ was not lacking before, and the Fall damaged but did not altogether destroy human nature. The acquisition of the finest pagan learning by the Christian will add enormously to his usefulness; 'how much the power of his virtue will be increased, more brilliantly and more widely known as if a torch had been set before it'. But moral worth without learning 'will die with its possessor, unless it be commended to posterity in written works'. He is even prepared to compare the usefulness of martyrs and scholars: 'The martyrs died, and so diminished the number of Christians; the scholars persuaded others and so increased it. In short, the martyrs would have shed their blood in vain for the teaching of Christ unless the others had defended it against the heretics by their writings.' (A 83)

In defence of his views, Batt invokes the famous testimony of Jerome and Augustine, although these were perhaps less favourable to his cause than one might believe from reading Erasmus. He invokes Jerome's analogy of the captive slave woman cleansed and turned into a daughter of Israel, to insist that 'we should not run away from any heathen literature, but should hand it over, cleansed, to Christian learning' (A 92–3). From Augustine he cites the classic metaphor of the Hebrews taking spoils from the Egyptians for their own use. Implied in this is the rejection of what is evil and superstitious. 'But if there is among them any gold of wisdom, any silver of speech, any furniture of good learning, we should pack up all that baggage and turn it to our own use, never fearing to be accused of thieving, but rather venturing to hope for reward and praise for the finest of deeds.' (A 97)

The last serious challenge to Batt's argument is the stark truth that, as the founders of the Christian religion, God chose unlettered apostles whom, surely, we should wish to emulate? Batt replies that while it is most desirable to imitate the apostles in faith, we should also imitate in learning the finest of the doctors of the Church, among whom Jerome is pre-eminent. What is more, Peter, with greater authority, consented to be instructed by Paul, the most highly educated among the apostles. Paul, alone possessing liberal learning, stands out among the other apostles as fitted to bear arms against the schools of Athens, 'and to range Roman eloquence under the sway of Christ'. Significantly, Batt cannot resist pointing out further that the supposedly rustic John was capable of 'that sublime utterance, ''In the beginning was the Word, and the Word was with God, and the Word was God.'' ' (A 103) Of this we shall have more to say. Batt also admits, more soberly, that 'it was not for nothing that it was arranged for the Christian religion to take its beginnings from untutored founders. That indeed was right, and its purpose was that the glory of such an event should not appertain to human effort but be attributed entirely to divine power.' (A 113) That was appropriate to those times, but what of the present? The apostles surely never reproved secular learning, and today, it is desperately important to meet the needs of Christendom.

The stylistic authority of this work (as of other among his early letters and writings), its classical citations and allusions, its vivacity and ease, betray not only unusual gifts but, already, a remarkable erudition. This would become increasingly apparent as time passed and Erasmus took responsibility for his own instruction in putting together the *Adagia*, not to mention the editions of Jerome and the New Testament. It is also clear that he was possessed of a prodigious memory. There is charming allusion to this evidently notorious gift in the opening pages of the *Antibarbari* when the fictional Batt, persuaded to give voice to his concerns, agrees to do so only if his remarks are kept in confidence by his friends, and also, 'if only Erasmus can be got to give his pen a rest. Whatever he even dreams at night he blackens his paper with in the daytime.' Erasmus points out that he has with him neither pen nor paper. 'Quite so,' replies Batt, 'but I know what a memory you have—it is as good as a notebook to you.' (A 40–1)

There is nothing mysterious about his educational masters: they are those of antiquity, Quintilian and Cicero among the foremost. Following thereon, inevitably, is the *De doctrina christiana* of Augustine. All are cited in the *Antibarbari* and frequently in his educational writings. Of course this is only the nucleus, since he seems to have come as near as anyone in his day might have done to fulfilling the mandate of the grammarian—the mastery of all known literature, in order properly to understand the use of speech. We recall the doctrine of a forgotten world, a rhetorical ideal of education, inherited by the Romans from the Greeks, and passed on into Christian antiquity chiefly by the Stoic writers. It conceived of education as directed to the formation of the whole individual, in intellect, and in morals. Its end was the virtuous man, fully informed about the experience of the past, nourished by knowledge of history's great achievements and tragedies, of the legacy of philosophy and literature, and devoted to the use of his talents for the good of the whole community. It is the ideal of the *doctus orator*, the learned orator, where *doctus* implies moral integrity as well as 'book learning'. It was Augustine's contribution in the *De doctrina* to build a bridge between this Ciceronian ideal and Christianity, to domesticate the life of the informed and virtuous pagan in the new religious world. His treatise was the vade-mecum for all of the Christian humanists.

For them, of course, the formative texts of the faith were added to the learning of antiquity. Scripture came first, but this was followed by the chief exponents among the Fathers of the Church, where Jerome and Augustine were foremost in learning

and authority. Toward the conclusion of the *Antibarbari* there is
a list of Christian writers who meet with approval: Augustine,
Jerome, Lactantius Firmianus, Ambrose, Bernard of Clairvaux,
Hilary of Poitiers, Bede ('even-toned and dull, but learned, considering his century'), and Gregory the Great. (A 105) The subject of the discussion is 'church writers and their eloquence',
but the list reveals more; it reveals an entire tradition of
theology, a tradition in which Erasmus most unmistakably
stands as a late if eminent figure.

At the heart of that tradition was an ancient conception of
wisdom, invoked by Erasmus at a critical point in the *Antibarbari*, where Batt is distinguishing genuine theologians from
those who 'grow old over a stack of jumbled anthologies and
digests, thinking nothing learned unless it is barbarous'. By
contrast he recommends 'the wise Ecclesiasticus: "the wise
man will seek out the wisdom of all the ancients, and will be
occupied with the prophets. He will keep the discourse of men
of renown, and will enter in among the subtleties of parables. He
will seek out the hidden meaning of proverbs, and be conversant
in the dark sayings of parables. He will serve among great men,
and appear before him that ruleth. He will travel through the
land of strange nations; he will try good and evil in all things." '
It is in the nature of such wisdom to join together the knowledge
of things human and divine as did the wisdom of Solomon, who
is also invoked with the approbation of Jerome: 'In the introduction to the Book of Proverbs he admonishes us to understand
words of prudence, subtleties of language, parables and dark
speeches, sayings of the sages, and riddles, which properly
belong to the dialecticians and philosophers.' (A 92)

Here we have the foundation of what Batt praises as 'no confused or barren erudition, but one which is polished and rich,
and founded in high antiquity' and we must recall that for
Erasmus and his friends, the true theology was the 'old
theology'. The wisdom on which it is founded is older than time
itself, a direct gift of God, as was that of Solomon. The text of
Genesis in the second chapter provides a clue: 'Out of the
ground the lord God formed every beast of the field and every
bird of the air, and brought them to the man to see what he
would call them; and whatever the man called every living

15

creature, that was its name.' So the naming of creatures was a divine power bestowed on Adam, a mark of his primordial understanding of the true nature of things and, individually, of their true *natures* which, of course, their names expressed. We find the same conception put by Plato: 'For the gods must clearly be supposed to call things by their right and natural names.'

The naming of creatures by the representative of the human family was therefore a sign in ancient tradition of man's mastery over all of creation to which he alone, among God's creatures, had the key: this was divine power. If God alone could utter the creative Word, which had the power to bring into being what it expressed, only his human creature, made in his image, had in turn the power of apprehension, signified by this ability to name. This power rested upon the response of man's created intellect to that to which it was akin, the mind of God, reflected also in all creation. And the greatest deprivation of that primordial cataclysm which we know as the Fall was the darkening of the human intellect, now alienated from its creator, so that it was no longer able to penetrate the inwardness of God's creation, which in turn was reduced to disorder by that same cataclysm.

As we have seen, however, that disorder was not complete. The ineffable God could still be discerned, if only dimly, through the darkened mirror of his creation, so that the wisdom of the ancients, and the tested experience of the race (to be discovered in parables and proverbs) were part of an authentic legacy. Moreover, if the glass had been darkened by the Fall, Christ, the new Adam, had done much to remedy the situation. Was he not the incarnate Word, one with the creative Word from before the beginning of time, identified with the Wisdom which had instructed Solomon and the prophets? Through grace and the power of rebirth in Christ, a better vision could be obtained, especially for those practised in holiness. On the level of morals and practical judgement, proverbial wisdom was a lifeline to supplement the teaching of revelation. The opening of the Book of Proverbs, referred to a moment ago, tells us that these proverbs were collected, 'that men may know wisdom and instruction, understand words of insight, receive instruction in wise dealing, righteousness, justice and equity, that prudence may be given to the simple, knowledge and discretion to the youth. . . . The fear of the Lord is the beginning of knowledge; fools despise wisdom and understanding.'

In these beliefs we have the essential key to an understanding of Erasmus' enterprise in all of its aspects. They explain the singular emphasis on the Word and on words, on speech and eloquence. Education in 'genuine letters'—*bonae litterae*—derives its regenerative power finally from the Word, to the degree that it is vested in traditions stemming from authentic wisdom. It must also now be grounded upon the Word incarnate revealed in the sacred page—in scripture—as well as the rhetorical word of ancient civil society. It must be directed by teachers of high moral character, themselves the product of such training, and for those who wished to apply themselves to the divine mysteries, the original languages were essential, since they alone could open the unpolluted springs of the primordial wisdom and experience of the race.

At the very conclusion of the *Antibarbari*, Batt leaves one question unanswered: 'It remains for us to refute those who say that it is not for a Christian to pay attention to eloquence.' Having to his own satisfaction made the case for the legitimacy of appropriating the wisdom of the past for Christian use, he admits, 'Those who condemn the study of eloquence are many in number, and they have perhaps something to say, if not true at least plausible.' (A 121) It is into this issue that we shall now follow Erasmus in his own voice, to learn why the mastery of eloquence by those capable of it was indeed indispensable to the Christian life.

2 The educational mission

Antibarbari is our most important source, at least for Erasmus' personal development, about the years spent in the monastery in Steyn. The surviving letters from that time are highly conventional exercises in epistolary style, and none at all survive from the last two or three years. We see only an Erasmus avid for literary studies and resentful of the 'barbarism' which is attacked in the *Antibarbari*, whose tones and attitudes are entirely supported by these few letters. In one, he lists his 'authorities in poetry'—Virgil, Horace, Ovid, Juvenal, Statius, Martial, Claudian, Persius, Lucan, Tibullus, and Propertius; in prose, Cicero, Quintilian, Sallust, and Terence. For style, he turns to Lorenzo Valla and to Rudolph Agricola, who was clearly his early inspiration among the northern humanists. After his ordination to the priesthood by the Bishop of Utrecht in 1492, he was permitted to take the post of Latin secretary to Hendrick van Bergen, bishop of Cambrai, who in the next year was named Chancellor of the Order of the Golden Fleece. Both bishops were well-educated, well-connected men of noble family, and Erasmus admired the pastoral and personal qualities of David of Burgundy, his ordaining bishop. From Hendrick van Bergen he presumably looked for further opportunity to study, especially since the bishop was hoping for a red hat, which posed the prospect of a visit to Italy. His hopes however were dashed, and, with them, Erasmus' expectations. Erasmus' letters become gloomy and fretful, and he speaks of 'endless distractions' which keep him from letter-writing and his studies. It is clear that with the assistance of Jacob Batt, who was influential with the bishop's family, he was allowed to go at last to university, to Paris, with the expressed intention of securing a doctor's degree in theology. The year was 1495. Except for occasional visits home, the next four years were spent in Paris, only the first of them at the Collège de Montaigu, where he found the life intolerable. By 1497 he was compelled to take pupils to support his studies. His educational programme germinated in this atmosphere, while he was giving lessons to young men who seem to have been foreigners in Paris, like himself. We have letters from Erasmus to Christian and Henrich Northoff, sons of a merchant from Lübeck, and to two young Englishmen of good family, Thomas Grey and Robert Fisher. Fisher was a kinsman of the future bishop, John Fisher, who was then chaplain and confessor to the Lady Margaret Beaufort and Master of Michaelhouse, Cambridge, and who was later to play an important part in Erasmus' career. The idea of providing teaching materials and helps to study for schoolboys in their assault on the Latin language would have come to Erasmus naturally enough, and in his letters to his pupils in Paris we find authors and precepts recommended also in his treatise on 'The Method of Study'—the *De ratione studii*, published by Erasmus in 1512. His epitome of Lorenzo Valla's *Elegantiae linguae latinae*, first composed for a schoolmaster while Erasmus was still at Steyn, was revised and expanded at this time, and he continued to lend the text to his friends. Valla's work was a landmark in humanist philology, first appearing in the 1440s and widely circulated thereafter. Erasmus finally brought out his paraphrase after his earlier version was published in 1529, without his knowledge, in Cologne and Paris. His revised and authorized version was published in Freiburg in 1531; nevertheless like many of his later publications it began at Steyn and in Paris.

Another of his principal works, on the acquisition of a rich rhetorical style, was in existence at least by 1499 as a manuscript entitled 'A brief instruction on abundance of style'— *Brevis de copia praeceptio*. This was in effect the first draft of what came to be the *De copia verborum ac rerum*—'Foundations of the Abundant Style', finally published in Paris in 1512. Other of his educational aids began to take shape. For the Northoffs he composed a small handbook of useful and polite conversation (there were many examples by others), 'Rules for familiar conversation', which grew eventually into one of his best-known and best-loved works, the *Colloquia*, or 'Colloquies'. For Robert Fisher he wrote the first version of his extensive treatise on the composition of Latin letters, *De conscribendis epistolis*. All of these works, like those written shortly after specifically for St Paul's school in London, and like his later

19

translation of the first two books of Theodore of Gaza's important Greek grammar, were intended in the first place to supply the want of sound instruction in the foundations of fine and fluent Latin and Greek. While of itself such an aim has a limited appeal, we must remember that eloquence was perhaps the foremost objective of the educational philosophy espoused by Erasmus and his colleagues. Without it, the informed and moral person could not be an effective, persuasive presence in Christian society.

Of all the works conceived and initiated during the Paris years, the one most informative for us is the *De ratione studii*. It is heavily indebted to Quintilian's *Institutio oratoria*, and also to Lorenzo Valla. It provides not only an account of how to organize study, and how to ensure a mastery of the authors deemed essential to the equipment of the effective citizen, but also how to keep such learning at hand. All authors are to be annotated, and the pupil is to collect notebooks of aphorisms and proverbs he finds striking and useful while reading his authors.

Since a true foundation must be laid, Erasmus wrote, 'Grammar claims primacy of place and at the outset boys must be instructed in two—Greek, of course, and Latin. This is not only because almost everything worth learning is set forth in these two languages, but in addition because each is so cognate to the other that both can be more quickly assimilated when they are taken in conjunction . . .' (S 667). The voice of the schoolmaster is sure and direct. The authors studied should be very limited in number 'but carefully chosen': Theodore of Gaza, followed (in second place) by Constantine Lascaris. The fourth-century grammarian Diomedes is recommended 'among ancient Latinists', but Erasmus finds little to choose among the more recent, excepting only Niccolo Perotti, secretary to Cardinal Bessarion and a member of the distinguished literary circle which included Theodore of Gaza and Lascaris. His *Rudimenta grammatices*, printed in Rome in 1473, was the first modern Latin grammar. In any case, Erasmus is reluctant to multiply the names of printed grammars, and it seems certain that he would rely principally on the teacher. He disagrees 'with the common run of teachers who, in inculcating these authors, hold boys back for several years'. No doubt his own experience was in his mind, but we must remember also that he is concerned above all that the young pupil should be taught to speak correctly, a skill 'best fostered both by conversing and consorting with those who speak correctly and by the habitual reading of the best stylists'. For the beginner he recommends Lucian, then Demosthenes, and thirdly, Herodotus. Among the poets, Aristophanes first, Homer second, and Euripides. Among Latin writers, Terence is first and foremost; 'he is pure, concise, and closest to everyday speech'. His subject-matter is also congenial to the young. He would add a few, well-selected comedies of Plautus, 'free from impropriety'. Virgil occupies the second place, then in order, Horace, Cicero, and finally Caesar. He would not object to the addition of Sallust. 'These, then, I believe to be sufficient for a knowledge of each language.' (S 669)

Once a pure linguistic foundation is laid, the youthful mind must be directed toward 'an understanding of things' as well as of words. Some of this will be absorbed in the course of reading the authors already listed, and almost all is to be sought in the Greek authors.

Further study with such masters as Lorenzo Valla will instruct the student in elegant style; he must also memorize the rules of poetry, and the chief points of rhetoric. Whenever reading, passages are to be marked at any striking word or expression, brilliance of argument or style, any adage, historical parallel, or maxim worth committing to memory. At the same time, 'the best master of style is the pen and you must therefore give it plenty of practice in poetry, prose and every sort of literary material' (S 671). The memory must also be cultivated, and while Erasmus does not disapprove of memory systems, he asserts, 'nevertheless, the best memory is based on three things above all: understanding, system and care. For memory largely consists in having thoroughly understood something.' Things which are necessary but difficult to remember may be written 'as briefly and attractively as possible on charts and hung up on the walls of a room where they are generally conspicuous'. The beginnings and ends of books will be likewise adorned with 'brief but pithy sayings', while other such will be inscribed on

21

rings or drinking cups, painted on doors and walls or even in the glass of a window so that what may aid learning is constantly before the eye. Finally, the greatest instruction of all comes from teaching others. 'For there is no better means of grasping what you understand and what you do not. Sometimes new ideas occur to one in preparing a lesson, and everything is more firmly fixed in the mind when teaching.' (S 672)

Accordingly, Erasmus concludes his treatise by considering the method of teaching pupils. Quintilian is again acknowledged as the master, 'so that it would seem the height of impertinence to write about a subject he has already dealt with' (S 672). Preparation of the teacher is first: he must have a firm grasp of the fundamentals of each discipline. Erasmus is in accord with the principles of the ancient grammarians, who insisted that a complete knowledge of all literature was needed if the understanding of any given word in its place was to be complete. He insists that the teacher must have much more than the usual 'select list' of authors at his command. 'He must range through the entire spectrum of writers so that he reads, in particular, all the best, but does not fail to sample any author, no matter how pedestrian.' Accordingly, he should have at hand his commonplace books where he notes 'systems and topics, so that wherever something noteworthy occurs he may write it down in the appropriate column' (S 672). An account of the commonplace book, which became one of the great conventions of learning in the two centuries that followed, is set forth at more length in the *De copia*, which was published together with the *De ratione studii*. Above all, Erasmus insists, 'recourse must be had to the sources themselves, that is, to the Greeks and the ancients. Plato, Aristotle, and his pupil Theophrastus will serve as the best teachers of philosophy, and then there is Plotinus who combines both these schools. Among theological writers, after the Scriptures, no one writes better than Origen, no one more subtly or attractively than Chrysostom, no one more devoutly than Basil. Among the Latin Fathers, two at least are outstanding in this field: Ambrose who is wonderfully rich in metaphors, and Jerome who is immensely learned in the sacred Scriptures.' In studying the poets it will also be necessary to command a good supply of mythological lore, 'and from whom is it better to seek this than Homer, the father of all myth?' The *Metamorphoses* and *Fasti* of Ovid are recommended, 'although written in Latin', as of no small importance. Geography, needed for history and poetry both, can be learned from Pomponius Mela, Ptolemy ('most eruditely'), and Pliny ('most comprehensively'). (S 673)

In this passage we find crystallized Erasmus's view of education as a grammarian: the totality of all good learning includes not only the ancient pagan masters, but scripture and the doctors of the Church. This is a single fabric, woven in many hues and from more than one fibre, but it is the fabric of Christian culture, from which the adornment of men and nations must, he holds, be fashioned. In his final sentence, he addresses the French friend to whom the work was dedicated as follows: 'Forge ahead as you have begun; apply yourself zealously to the cause of learning, and adorn your native France, so illustrious in other spheres, with ennobling studies as well.' (S 691) It is too easy to read such words as mere convention and dismiss them, but the intent was serious and, in the author's mind, the cause the most urgent and fundamental of any facing the nations of Europe. For reasons indicated in the previous chapter, education in the works of worthy authors, both sacred and profane, was an immersion in the mystery of the Word, an ascesis that cleansed the soul and turned the nature of the learner to good and holy ends.

We left Erasmus with his pupils in Paris, among them two Englishmen, Thomas Grey and Robert Fisher. By November 1498, he was also acting as tutor to William Blount, fourth Baron Mountjoy, whose grandfather had been ennobled by Henry VI for loyal service during the Wars of the Roses. Mountjoy became a patron and firm friend, and the next year he invited Erasmus to accompany him when he returned to England. This first stay was brief, but it may have been during that visit, in conversation with Mountjoy, that Erasmus conceived of another work which was, in time, to become a cornerstone of the revived classical culture of Europe, the *Adagia*. Once again, Paris and the circle of pupils there provided the place and occasion; the first version was published there in 1500 with a prefatory letter dedicating the work to Lord Mountjoy. It was called the *Adagiorum collectanea*, and it contained 818 adages, Greek and Latin. Like the *De copia*, it emerged directly from Erasmus practising what he preached, and from edition to edition it grew abundantly with the passage of time. It is the centrepiece of Erasmus' secular learning, and occupied the same position in that sphere of knowledge and understanding as did the edition of the New Testament in sacred learning. Some explanation of it is therefore essential in this place.

In his dedicatory letter to Mountjoy, Erasmus explains, with pleasing fiction, that the work came about when he set aside more serious studies owing to a fever, 'and strolled through divers gardens of the classics, occupied in this lighter kind of study, and so plucked, and as it were arranged in garlands, like flowerets of every hue, all the most ancient and famous of the adages'. And he hopes as well that the collection will be of use to others, 'those, I mean, who dislike the current jargon and are searching for greater elegance and a more refined style' (W 1.257).

The printer of this modest book of 152 pages was a German named Master Johann Philipp, who had set up his presses on the south bank of the Seine, near the Collège de Montaigu and the Abbey of Sainte-Geneviève, in a district well known to Erasmus. The printer's blurb described it as 'A collection of *paroemiae* or adages, old and most celebrated, made by Desyderius Herasmus Roterdamus: a work both new and wonderfully useful for conferring beauty and distinction on all kinds of speech and writing'. The book was printed in Roman type, to identify its kinship with Italian humanism. It was a book of Latin scholarship—Erasmus was still struggling to master Greek—but it provided Greek versions for 154 of the proverbs it contained and 143 more were added in the second edition. It was thus one of the first books issued from the Paris presses to print some words in Greek, which in itself gave it great cachet. The *Collectanea* would be of small intrinsic importance if it had not been the seed from which a massive achievement would grow, yet to the literary circles in Paris and England it was a landmark. In 1508 it re-emerged in wholly new form as from a chrysalis, as the *Adagiorum Chiliades* ('ordered in thousands'), a book beautifully printed by Aldus in Venice, in which the number of

adages had risen to 3,260. This version reflected Erasmus'
reading of the Greek authors since 1500, containing a large
proportion of Greek passages, and its aim was not simply to
explain the proverb,but to give its whole pedigree, as the saying
moved from author to author, from poetry to prose. The proverb
was also a convenient peg, quite often, on which to hang pictur-
esque information about the ancient world, or telling commentary about the issues of the day. It was this possibility which led
to some of the adages taking on an independent literary existence of their own. The Froben edition of 1515 envisaged a yet
wider public, added new adages and long commentaries, and
Latin translations of all the Greek. The process of enrichment
continued in the edition of 1517/18 and in each of the six editions up to that of 1536. At Erasmus' death in that year, the
number of adages was 4,151.

In his introduction to the *Adagia* Erasmus opens with the
topic 'What a proverb is'. He first cites the Latin grammarian,
Donatus, as follows: 'A proverb is ''a saying which is fitted to
things and times''. Diomedes however defines it as follows: ''A
proverb is the taking over of a popular saying, fitted to things
and times, when the words say one thing and mean another.'' '
Then, noting that many definitions exist among the Latin and
Greek writers, Erasmus sums up the leading elements on which
there is agreement: a proverb has in it something of the allegory,
and it contains something gnomic or didactic, which is helpful
in the conduct of life. Despite the great variety, he continues, 'I
would not deny that the majority of adages have some kind of
metaphorical disguise. I think the best of them are those which
equally give pleasure by their figurative colouring and profit by
the value of their ideas.' He proposes then a complete definition
of his own: 'A proverb is a saying in popular use, remarkable for
some shrewd and novel turn.' (Ad 4)

In this passage, 'proverb' represents the Greek *paroemia*,
which we read also in the printer's blurb advertising the *Collectanea*. The term could mean a byword, but it could also carry
the sense of an enigma or parable. When the disciples of Jesus
say that their master is now speaking plainly and not in any
figure (John 16: 29), the Greek word is *paroemia*. There may be
something numinous, therefore, about an adage, which, like an

25

analogy, alludes to more than it signifies directly. Erasmus emphasizes the antiquity of proverbs, and how they were respected by the greatest among the ancients, from Aristotle and Plato through Plutarch and the poets, even to their use by Christ himself: 'by their fruits shall ye know them', 'they strain at a gnat and swallow a camel'. They encapsulate ancient wisdom and the experience of the race, and 'there appears to be no form of teaching which is older than the proverb. In these symbols, as it were, almost all the philosophy of the Ancients was contained. What were the oracles of those wise old Sages but proverbs? They were so deeply respected in old time that they seemed to have fallen from heaven rather than to have come from men. 'And *Know thyself* descended from the sky', says Juvenal.' (Ad 13)

This primordial quality is of course of the greatest interest to Erasmus. He is prepared to hint that proverbs derive from that time of ancient harmony and understanding before the cataclysm of our first parents. In explaining why he has said that they belong to the science of philosophy, he states that 'Aristotle, according to Synesius, thinks that proverbs were simply the vestiges of that earliest philosophy which was destroyed by the calamities of human history'. For that reason they are to be looked into, 'closely and deeply: for underlying them there are what one might call sparks of that ancient philosophy, which was much more clear-sighted in its investigation of truth than were the philosophers who came after. Plutarch too . . . thinks the adages of the Ancients very similar to the rites of religion, in which things which are most important and even divine are often expressed in ceremonies of a trivial and seemingly almost ridiculous nature.' (Ad 14) He suggests that these sayings, brief as they are, give a hint in their concealed way of those very things which were propounded in so many volumes by the princes of philosophy. For instance, that proverb in Hesiod, 'The half is more than the whole', is exactly what Plato in the *Gorgias* and in his books on the State tries to expound by so many arguments: it is preferable to receive an injury than to inflict one. What doctrine was ever produced by the philosophers more salutary as a principle of life or closer to the Christian religion?

This is a chord struck again and again throughout the entirety of the *Adagia*: the explicit desire to show the harmony between classical wisdom and Christian teaching. In the passage immediately following that above, Erasmus cites Pythagoras, 'Between friends all is common'. This is the first of the entire collection, and Erasmus hails this as enclosing in a brief saying the whole of human happiness. 'What other purpose has Plato in so many volumes except to urge a community of living and the factor which creates it, namely friendship? If only he could persuade mortals of these things, war, envy and fraud would at once vanish from our midst; in short a whole regiment of woes would depart from life once and for all. What other purpose had Christ, the prince of our religion? One precept and one alone He gave to the world, and that was love; on that alone, He taught, hang all the law and the prophets. Or what else does love teach us, except that all things should be common to all? In fact that united in friendship with Christ, glued to Him by the same binding force that holds Him fast to the Father, imitating so far as we may that complete communion by which He and the Father are one, we should also be one with Him, and as Paul says, should become one spirit and one flesh with God, so that by the laws of friendship all that is His is shared with us and all that is ours is shared with Him; and then that, linked one to another in the same bonds of friendship, as members of one Head and like one and the same body we may be filled with the same spirit, and weep and rejoice at the same things together. This is signified to us by the mystic bread, brought together out of many grains into one flour, and the draught of wine fused into one liquid from many clusters of grapes. Finally, love teaches how, as the sum of all created things is in God and God is in all things, the universal all is in fact one. You see that an ocean of philosophy, or rather of theology, is opened up to us by this tiny proverb.' (Ad 15)

This abrupt flight into the most serious issues of the Christian faith is utterly characteristic of Erasmus, and it occurs equally in another, more controversial work which appeared not long after the publication of the *Chiliades*, the *Praise of Folly* (1511). Nothing gives more vivid witness to his personal vision of the unity of human understanding and experience.

The *Adagia* then found followers for many reasons. It was a treasury of stylistic adornments; it was, equally, a handbook of erudition in which the user, learned or not, could claim an acquaintance with the classical heritage to astonish and delight his readers. As a vade-mecum of ancient culture, it also provided a historical perspective on the past which distinguishes it from its medieval antecedents, the encyclopaedias and compendia of knowledge. Not that the *Adagia* professes to teach history. Its information about the past is fragmentary, although animated by Erasmus' critical sense and commentaries on his sources. At the same time it is unsystematic and disorganized, and filled with gossip, which gives its contents the savour of actuality. An example at random might be the adage *Frons occipitio prior*, 'Forehead before occiput'—the occiput being the back part of the head. Erasmus delights in the riddling quality of this ancient saw, finds it in Cato *On Agriculture*, chapter 4, in Pliny, and in Aristotle's *Economica*, Book 1, where it is used to mean that the presence of the master was the most important thing in the successful conduct of affairs. Erasmus is then reminded of a passage in Columella, of a story in Aulus Gellius, of a passage in Plutarch's essay 'On the Education of Children', and of the same simile used by Aeschylus in the *Persians*. He then proceeds through Livy and Terence to conclude as follows:

'The person who should most take note of this is the prince, if he really has the mind of a prince and not of a pirate, that is if he has the public good at heart. But in these days bishops and kings do everything through other people's hands, ears and eyes, and think the common good is what concerns them least, kept busy as they are with their own private possessions or entirely bent on pleasure.' (Ad 165)

There was probably no other work from Erasmus' hand which had a greater direct impact on European culture than this, nor one more difficult to trace. A glance through an index of the *Adagia* will reveal phrases that are still on our lips, which many would probably attribute, vaguely, to the Bible, and which almost none would know had once been put abroad in Erasmus' great compilation: A necessary evil; There's many a slip 'twixt cup and lip; To squeeze water out of a stone; To leave no stone unturned; Let the cobbler stick to his last; God helps those who help themselves; The grass is greener over the fence; The cart before the horse; Dog in the manger; One swallow doesn't make a summer; His heart was in his boots; A rare bird; To have one foot in the grave; To be in the same boat; To sleep on it; To call a spade a spade; Up to the ears; To break the ice; Ship-shape; To die of laughing; To have an iron in the fire; To look a gift horse in the mouth; Neither fish nor flesh; Like father, like son; Not worth a snap of the fingers; He blows his own trumpet; To show one's heels. (Ph 7)

From time to time Erasmus ordered his writings into categories, with the thought in mind that one day they would be published as a whole, as indeed they were immediately on his death. The categories include educational works, *moralia* (including *Praise of Folly*), works of piety, and the many *apologiae* which he wrote to respond to his critics. Two large items in his legacy fit into none of these classes, and he listed them separately between the educational and the moral writings. One of these is the body of his letters: the second, the *Adagia*. The *Adagia* were indeed a hybrid, partly a work of literary instruction, partly the work of a moralist, partly touching on religion and piety. He explained to Colet that they came about as a by-product of his studies in Greek literature, preparatory to his study of the New Testament. There is no reason to doubt this, and it was utterly characteristic that, with his restless intellect and pen, he saw the opportunity to create a remarkable new work that would remain, not quite incidentally, a valuable commonplace book for his own use. Although he intended in principle to exclude from it proverbs in scripture, he could not resist the inclusion of some, as we have seen. We have drawn attention to his conviction that there was a genuine link between the culture represented by the classics and that revealed by God in Christ. As a grammarian, he knew that it would not be possible to understand the one without a complete grasp of the other. It is time, then, to turn to the enterprise for which the *Adagia* and many of the related educational works were really in part a propaedeutic, and that is the study of the Fathers and the New Testament.

3 Adorning the temple of the Lord

Erasmus' edition of the New Testament, which made the Greek text available in print for the first time, is remembered as his most important achievement. This is partly because his profound influence in other spheres, especially in education and Christian piety, became virtually invisible by its general absorption into the mainstream of European thought: the presence of his *Adages* throughout the works of Shakespeare is an illustrative example. Nevertheless the symbolic importance of the *Novum instrumentum* (as he called it initially) in defining the impact of Christian humanism on the intellectual culture of the day is matched by that of no other single work, including his own *Praise of Folly*. The fact that the *editio princeps* of 1516 became (rightly or wrongly) notorious for its errors, that its very status as an edition was unclear even to his contemporaries, and that its absorption into the *textus receptus* of biblical scholarship contributed to a legacy of critical problems that were not unravelled until the advent of 'higher criticism' in the nineteenth century—all of these serious qualifications notwithstanding, where the name of Erasmus is remembered, it is remembered first for the printing of the New Testament in Greek.

A new generation of scholars has given us for the first time a proper understanding of the curious inception of this famous work, and of its true nature. It is now clear that the printing of the Greek text was, in the strict sense, the last thing that mattered. Moreover, attention to it as an *editio princeps* has diverted attention away from the other two components making up the *Novum instrumentum*, a new Latin version of the text revising the Vulgate, and an assembly of copious notes known as the *Annotations*. These were not footnotes, but rather an independent work which is actually an extended commentary, not on the Greek, but on the Vulgate *textus receptus* of the day. Of the three elements contained in the *Novum instrumentum*—the Greek text, the Latin translation, and the

Annotations—only the last was a part of his original project. In order to understand how all of this came about, and to make a proper assessment of the importance of his New Testament scholarship in the wider enterprise of the Dutch humanist, we must return to that critical period at the end of Erasmus' stay in the University of Paris.

In 1499, we recall, Erasmus accompanied Lord Mountjoy to England, at a time when he was occupied with the incipient *Adages* and the *Antibarbari*. He spent the best part of a year there, from the spring of 1499 until January 1500. The visit provided him with many valuable introductions, not least to Thomas More and, through him, to the youthful Prince Henry, who was to become Henry VIII. Most important of all was his stay in Oxford at the house of studies of his religious order, the Augustinian canons. This was St Mary's College, not far from the Oxford Castle in what is now New Inn Hall Street. He seems to have spent the Michaelmas term there. The prior of St Mary's, Richard Charnock, was a sympathetic colleague who joined with Mountjoy in urging Erasmus to persevere with what was to be the *Collectanea*, the first version of the *Adages*. John Colet had been lecturing in the university for some time on the Epistles of St Paul, bringing to them his considerable knowledge of Florentine Neoplatonism and, presumably, other resources from an earlier education of which we know but little. His lectures, although from the traditional Vulgate text, apparently inspired Erasmus as they inspired other of his hearers, by deriving theological reflection directly from scripture and the Fathers, rather than from scholastic reasoning. The method was not new; it was that of the 'old theology' practised by the authorities whom Erasmus cited in the *Antibarbari*, and which continued after the birth of scholasticism like an underground stream among the Victorines and in monastic schools. Nevertheless, to the members of Colet's university audience at Oxford in the last years of the fifteenth century, his approach came as a revelation of new possibilities, especially in combination with the newly fashionable Neoplatonism from Florence.

Colet's impact on Erasmus must be inferred from a half-dozen surviving letters. Initially, Erasmus presented himself modestly to Colet as one who 'enjoys but little experience of letters, but

31

admits to a consuming passion for them', and who finds England most agreeable in that it is 'well supplied with that without which life itself is disagreeable to me; I mean men who are well versed in good literature' (W. 1.201). However, what Colet and Erasmus discuss, and with much seriousness, is theology, and in particular, the central issue of Jesus' awareness of his own humanity, and its implications for his suffering. It is most likely that Erasmus was caught up suddenly with a frustration which had pursued him through the monastery and the schools in Paris—the sterility (in his view) of the 'modern class of theologians, who spend their lives in sheer hair-splitting and sophistical quibbling'. If he had been indifferent to theology, a devotee of pagan learning and letters and nothing more, he would have been less indignant. His response to Colet's concerns is deeply serious, since (as he wrote) he regarded theology as, indeed, 'that great queen of all sciences, enriched and adorned as she had been by the eloquence of antiquity'. In his view, the adoption of Aristotelian logic as the necessary framework for theological sciences by the university masters had imposed on the religious wisdom of the past an alien, arcane, and speculative discipline which made it inaccessible to any but the specialists, and displaced the primary authority of the text of scripture with a pagan artifice. The 'modern' theologians therefore—the Scotists and Occamists—were seen by him 'to choke up, as it were with brambles, the way of a science that early thinkers had cleared and, attempting to settle all questions, so they claim, merely envelop all in darkness' (W 1.203).

It is not necessary then to suppose that up to this time Erasmus had been simply (in the words of one scholar) 'a divided personality, the unwilling monk obliged to pursue the study of scholastic theology, and the ardent wooer of the classical Muse'. He was too well acquainted with antiquity—that antiquity which included the first four centuries of Christian history—to think that there was no alternative to the scholasticism which he found so tedious and repugnant in the schools of Paris. As one brought up in the spiritual culture of the Netherlands, in contact with the 'modern devotion' through his schooling and his religious community, as an early student of Jerome and a lover of the 'Christian Virgil', Baptista

Mantuanus, he was already persuaded of the rhetorical and devotional nature of theology, supported by the tradition of the Church. It is entirely possible—indeed, likely—that not until his arrival in Oxford had he heard a theologian lecture in the manner of the 'old theology' who was also familiar with the latest enthusiasms of the classical revival, and who was therefore able to bring to life those deep affinities between classical antiquity and the Christian revelation of which Erasmus was already convinced.

This is important because of a persistent tradition that the conversion of Erasmus from poetry and elegant *belles-lettres* occurred only after his time at Paris, when he came to know the English humanists and, in particular, John Colet. We might recall an earlier correspondence with a fellow-Augustinian, Cornelis Gerard, an older man and a member of a house near Leiden. Like Erasmus he was a native of Gouda, and it is likely that their acquaintance was an early one. He was a man of letters who was crowned poet laureate by the Emperor Maximilian in 1508, and he is probably among those who gave Erasmus help and encouragement in his early studies. In the summer of 1489, writing to Gerard with his familiar complaints about those who condemn poetry as immoral ('. . . shall we have to censure for indecency everything that is wittily expressed or poetic?'), Erasmus invokes the authority of St Jerome: 'those worthies are only drawing a cloak over their own lack of culture, with the result that they seem to despise what they despair of achieving. If they looked carefully at Jerome's letters, they would see at least that lack of culture is not holiness, nor cleverness impiety.' (W 1.35) He also informed Gerard that he had not only read the letters of Jerome 'long ago', but copied out all of them with his own hands. It is evident that in the very years when Erasmus was discovering the Valla of the *Elegantiae* and the canon of authors in ancient Greece and Rome, he was also finding a model of Christian learning in that first master of the text of scripture, St Jerome.

As a result of their colloquies, Colet reproached Erasmus for having devoted his life entirely to secular literature. Erasmus was now in his early thirties. There was doubtless an element of self-justification in his reply. He insisted that those studies were an apprenticeship only. On the other hand, he was not yet ready to join Colet in the proper theological exposition of the Bible, and insisted that that task still lay ahead for him. He needed better preparation. In particular, he needed a mastery of Greek—a requirement which was not, it seems, so apparent to Colet. Erasmus returned to Paris to repair that want at all costs, and the first evidence of his enterprise, which was clearly already in hand before he went to England, was the Greek contained in the *Collectanea*, which appeared in the following July.

His apprenticeship was a long one, and it led through the legacy of his master, Jerome. Soon after his return to the Continent, Erasmus set out to restore and edit the letters of Jerome and to write a commentary on them. It was a great commitment, and one which combined his love of antiquity with his religion. To Jacob Batt, who was seeking financial support for Erasmus' project, he wrote that he hoped 'to restore the entire text of Jerome, which has been spoiled and garbled and confused by the ignorance of divines, for I have found many passages in his writings that are corrupt or spurious, and to restore the Greek. By so doing I shall cast light on the ancient world and illuminate his literary achievement, which I venture to say nobody hitherto has appreciated. . . . There will be no need for you to tell lies in this connexion, dear Batt, for I really am working at this.' (W. 1.305)

Writing to another friend at the same time, he denounces the neglect of Jerome. 'Great Heavens: Scotus and Albertus Magnus and still more unscholarly writers than these are noisily preached in every school, while Jerome, the supreme champion and expositor and ornament of our faith . . . is the only one among all the Fathers of whom no mention is made.' And why? 'That very excellence of style, which benefitted our faith, has done harm to its creator. Many are put off by the profound learning which ought to have been the especial source of his fame; so there are few to admire an author who is comprehended by few indeed.' (W 1.141) Enlarging upon his plans, he discloses an editorial procedure which was wholly indebted to the classical grammarians, and in future to be used in his ambitious programme for the restoration of the sources of Christianity, including the New Testament itself. First, he will purge

Jerome's text of the errors accumulated over the centuries. Secondly, he will examine the evidence for Jerome's own learning—his classical sources, his Greek scholarship, his knowledge of ancient history—as well as 'all those stylistic and rhetorical accomplishments in which he not only far outstrips all Christian writers, but even seems to rival Cicero himself'. In a word, he would treat Jerome as a historical figure, writing in a specific time and culture, who would express himself accordingly, and who could be understood properly only with a knowledge of that time and culture. This was what the humanist approach implied, important enough in studying ancient literature, but potentially very disturbing when applied to the great religious texts whose eternal verities had been abstracted by the philosophers from the concrete realities of the world in which they were conceived and set down.

Was this decision to edit the works of Jerome an evasion of his promise to devote the rest of his life to the study of scripture? Not in the least, although it is tempting to see in his affinity with Jerome something more than a shared concern to establish the text of scripture. Jerome's vivid letters, his ardent, passionate nature, his powerful affections and hostilities, his dislike of hypocrites, his self-condemnations, his combativeness—all of these call to mind the temperament of his great humanist admirer. Jerome too was in love, famously, with the pagan classics, and was torn by guilt over this addiction in the face of his equally powerful ascetic vocation; in this he felt more unease than did Erasmus. Erasmus had, however, one problem lacking to Jerome; he had to work in relation to an acknowledged, 'received' Latin text of the New Testament, where Jerome's task had been precisely to establish such a text. Everything points to the fact that it was this received Latin text—the Vulgate—which was the final object of Erasmus' concern. The road to it led, therefore, through Jerome. In Jerome's day there were several Latin versions in common use, some of which preserved important readings from Greek texts already lost. Jerome's new translation was made from the Greek, but incorporated important critical information retained in these 'Old Latin' versions, as they have come to be known. Jerome's text, which was accompanied by volumes of commentaries, came to be known as the 'Vulgate', or common text of Latin Christendom. Its Old Testament Jerome translated directly from the Hebrew, in place of the Greek 'Septuagint' version of the Hebrew Scriptures which was authoritative in his day. By Erasmus' time the Vulgate text had endured so many vagaries in its journey through the centuries that Erasmus declared it no longer represented Jerome's original version. His own efforts could therefore be seen in part as an extension of his editorial labours over Jerome himself.

If Erasmus were to achieve his aim of re-establishing Jerome's Latin translation of the New Testament, he had clearly to become familiar with the Greek versions which underlay it. By the same token, he had to attain the familiarity with Greek letters which would allow him to read the Greek New Testament with something of the authority that Jerome's understanding brought to it. These then are the continuing preoccupations of the years that follow his departure from Oxford.

When he returned to the Continent in 1500 he began to search for Greek texts of the Gospels and Psalms. He was also searching for a haven in which to continue his studies, since the plague at Paris and Orléans had driven him from both cities back to his native Holland, where in due course he settled at the castle of Tournehem with his friend Jacob Batt, now tutor to the young Adolph of Burgundy. Here he came into contact with an ecclesiastic whose influence on him was at least as powerful as that of John Colet—Jean Vitrier. Vitrier was an Observant Franciscan, a graduate of Louvain, and now Warden of the Franciscan convent at nearby Saint-Omer, where Vitrier had been born. He was heir to the Franciscan spiritualism of the previous century which had been touched by the apocalyptic doctrines of Joachim of Fiore. He was an intransigent reformer, a mystic influenced by Origen, and an opponent of the scholastic method. After a perhaps predictably difficult beginning, the relationship between the two men deepened with their discovery of common concerns, and in particular, Vitrier encouraged Erasmus' study of St Paul, and his appreciation of Origen. During a retreat at Courtebourne Erasmus read Origen's homilies and his commentary on the Epistle to the Romans. One immediate result was the composition of the *Enchiridion*,

Erasmus' first great essay in devotional literature, which was infused with citations from Origen.

By this time, Erasmus had already decided to write his own commentary on the Epistle to the Romans, a classic undertaking for a devotee of the 'old theology'. He sought from the library at the abbey of St Bertin in nearby Saint-Omer the commentaries of Augustine, Ambrose, and Nicholas of Lyra, as well as Origen 'or anyone else who has written a commentary on Paul'. In his dedicatory preface to the *Enchiridion*, written in the autumn of 1501, he referred to his project in terms now familiar to us, as something 'to cause certain malicious critics, who think it the height of piety to be ignorant of sound learning, to realize that, when in my youth I embraced the finer literature of the ancients and acquired, not without much midnight labour, a reasonable knowledge of the Greek as well as the Latin language, I did not aim at vain glory or childish self-gratification, but had long ago determined to adorn the Lord's temple, badly desecrated as it has been by the ignorance and barbarism of some, with treasures from other realms' (W 2.53). Three years later he informed Colet that he had finished four volumes of this work 'at one rush, as it were', but interrupted himself because he needed Greek 'at every point'. He also took up the study of Hebrew, 'but stopped because I was put off by the strangeness of the language, and at the same time the shortness of life'. As for Origen, he informed Colet that 'he reveals some of the wellsprings, as it were, and demonstrates some of the basic principles, of the science of theology' (W 2.87). It would be interesting to know what Colet made of all this. He certainly did not agree with Erasmus' insistence on the value of knowing the masters of pagan literature for scriptural study, as Erika Rummel has said. In his lectures on Corinthians he repudiated this view directly, asking whether such reliance 'does not make them a chief obstacle to such understanding', since in reading the pagan authors for assistance, 'you distrust your power of understanding the Scriptures by grace alone, and prayer, and by the help of Christ, and of faith' (R 12).

In 1504, in the abbey of Parc just outside Louvain, Erasmus discovered a manuscript of Valla's notes on the text of the Vulgate, his *Collatio novi testamenti*. He published it the following year as *Adnotationes in novum testamentum*. His discovery of these notes would certainly have confirmed his philological interests, although Erasmus had already begun his task. Valla's was strictly a grammarian's appraisal, comparing a number of manuscripts, including the Greek, and preferring the earlier as more authoritative. He examined the grammatical and rhetorical elements in the formation of the Vulgate text, and criticized some obscurities of meaning. It was not the work of an exegete or a theologian, and Erasmus commented later that Valla's study was 'most praiseworthy' for his energy and method, and that he was 'a man more concerned with literature than with theology . . . although in some things I differ from him, especially in those that relate to theological science' (W 3.137). This letter, written in 1515, confirms the impression that Erasmus conceived of his responsibility as, finally, a theological one. In restoring the text of scripture, he would also initiate a renewal of Christian theology. His models in this mission were Jerome, Augustine, and Origen, all of whom he mentions repeatedly, but, above all, his model was Jerome.

It was long believed that his discovery of Valla's annotations on the New Testament was the immediate inspiration for his own Latin version, and that his work on this began in 1505–6. This belief rested on the existence of manuscript copies intended for Colet and for Henry VIII, and bearing dates of October 1506 and September 1509. These manuscripts contain the texts both of the Vulgate and of Erasmus' version. Thanks to the scholarship of Andrew Brown, it is now known that the colophon dates in these manuscripts, which were prepared by Pieter Meghen, a copyist much favoured in the English humanist circle, applied only to the Vulgate text contained in them, and that Erasmus' translation (in an Oxford manuscript, interlinear, in the others in a wide margin) was added in the 1520s. This discovery verifies Erasmus' own statements to the effect that he had no intention of preparing an entire reworking of the Vulgate text, and that the decision to add one was made at the last minute, after the work was already ready for Froben's press.

How, then, did Erasmus proceed? We left him with his work on Jerome, his writing of the *Enchiridion*, his editing of Valla's annotations on the New Testament, and his undertaking of a commentary on the Epistles of St Paul, arrested by his deficiencies in Greek. In 1505 he made a second trip to England. Translations from the Greek are the keynote: from Lucian, with Thomas More, from Euripides, now added to his earlier translations from the writings of the rhetorician Libanius, who numbered among his pupils St John Chrysostom, whom Erasmus greatly admired. These were practice pieces, and we must assume that, if his earlier explanations to Colet have something of a self-justifying air, these exercises fit precisely into his programme for self-education in Greek. In the spring of 1506 Erasmus left England for Italy, accompanying the sons of a Genoese physician who had settled in England, professedly 'mainly in order to learn Greek'. He was to spend the next three years in Italy, where he took, perfunctorily, a doctorate in theology from the University at Turin, and stayed with Aldus in Venice to complete a much augmented edition of the *Adagia* and to work on editions of Plautus, Terence, and Seneca's tragedies. His travels took him to Padua, Siena, and Rome, and then as far as Naples, whence he visited the cave of the Sibyl at Cumae. These years, and those that followed until the spring of 1511, are most obscure since no letter from his pen survives between December 1508 (to Aldo Manuzio in Venice) and April 1511 (to Andrea Ammonio, from Dover). He returned to England in 1509 on the accession of Henry VIII to the throne, and it is to this period that we owe the *Praise of Folly*. He is presumed to have lived in London during an extended period of which, again, we know nothing. The letter to Ammonio was written while Erasmus was on his way to Paris, to supervise the printing of the *Praise of Folly*. He returned to London by mid-June, and fell ill with the sweating sickness, from which he was still feeling the effects when he had to go to Cambridge to take up a position created for him by John Fisher, to lecture in Greek. He translated the Mass of St John Chrysostom from the Greek, and presented to Fisher a translation of St Basil's commentary on Isaiah. He lectured on the grammar of Manuel Chrysoloras and, for more senior listeners, on that of Theodore Gaza. He completed the *De copia*, written originally before he left for Italy, and amplified his treatise on letter-writing, the *De conscribendis epistolis*. His letters began to be sprinkled liberally with Greek phrases. In 1512, he dedicated to Archbishop Warham, who had presented him with the living of Aldington in Kent, a group of translations from Lucian. In all of this, no reference survives to his projected work on the Epistles of St Paul. From his later remarks we gather that he was seeking out Greek and Latin manuscripts to compare with the Vulgate, and in the autumn of 1512 he remarks, 'I intend to finish the revision of the New Testament and the letters of St Jerome; if I have time, I will also emend the text of Seneca.' The following July he informed Colet in a postcript that 'I have finished the collation of the New Testament and am now starting on St Jerome' (W 2.249).

In the scattered information contained in the few letters that survive up to the time Erasmus left England for Basle, in July 1514, we can see that his interest in Greek continued, and that he taught himself the language by his own methods—the study of a wide range of the best authors, the discipline of translation, and by editing texts. It is dangerous to argue from silence, so the fact that he says practically nothing about his work on the Vulgate itself need mean nothing more than that this was all one enterprise, and that the work on the Greek New Testament was part and parcel of his work on a revision of the Vulgate. By 1514 he had completed his 'collation'. When he approached the Froben press, what exactly did he have in hand?

The most recent scholarship suggests that Erasmus intended at that point to publish the Vulgate text of the New Testament with an extended commentary—the *Annotations*. Beatus Rhenanus, fully familiar with the world of printers in Basle and destined to become a close friend of Erasmus, wrote that Erasmus had arrived in Basle, 'weighed down with good books', including his revision of Jerome, the works of Seneca, also revised, a number of translations from Plutarch, a book of *Parallels* (the *Parabolae*), the *Adages*, and 'copious notes on the New Testament' (R 23). These were unprecedented in their scope and in their extensive, consistent references to Greek texts. To follow the conjecture of Erika Rummel, it was no doubt this that suggested a much larger enterprise to Froben, one that would bring particular fame to his press and demonstrate its capacity to set up in type an extended text in Greek: the Greek text of the

New Testament should be supplied also, along with Erasmus' annotations. This conjecture is supported by later statements of Erasmus himself, and by the contemporary remarks of Beatus Rhenanus. In August 1515 Erasmus informed Reuchlin personally that, 'I have written annotations on the entire New Testament, and so have now in mind to print the New Testament in Greek with my comments added.' At some point it was decided further not to print the Vulgate, but in its place a new Latin version by Erasmus, written in Basle (as he always maintained) under considerable pressure of time. His annotations however preserved his first intention, since they were cued not to Erasmus' new Latin text, but to the Vulgate which was not printed. In the first edition of 1516 the annotations were also printed quite apart from the Greek text and its parallel Latin translation. Of these three elements then—the Greek text, the Latin translation, and the *Annotations*—only the last was the product of a long and painstaking scholarly enterprise. At the same time, Erasmus' dedication to that task provided the firm foundation for his critical revision of the Vulgate, and explains why he was able to produce the text so swiftly. His personal conception of what had been done is discovered most succinctly in the long title with which the work is introduced, which, as has been observed, makes no mention of the fact that the Greek text had actually been printed for the first time. It describes: the *Novum instrumentum* revised and emended by Erasmus of Rotterdam, against the Greek original as well as many ancient manuscripts in both Latin and Greek, and against the evidences (quotations, emendations, and interpretations) to be found in the 'most approved' authors, especially Origen, Chrysostom, Cyril, Theophylact, Jerome, Cyprian, Ambrose, Hilary, and Augustine, together with Annotations which tell the reader 'what has been changed and why'. The whole is recommended to lovers of true theology, who are asked not to be offended by any changes they discover, but rather to think whether or not the text has been changed for the better.

If we ask what sources Erasmus used for his revision, it will be clear by now that we must distinguish between those consulted over many years in the preparation of his annotations and those actually used in printing the Greek text in Basle. For

41

this latter purpose, Erasmus made use of manuscripts in Basle which had been left to the Dominicans there by Cardinal Ivan Stojkovic of Ragusa, a delegate to the Council of Basle who had died in Lausanne in 1443. Erasmus presented Froben with a manuscript—not a transcription—supplied by the Dominicans, a twelfth-century text of the Gospels which survives today, containing Erasmus' emendations between the lines and in the margins, and the printer's red chalk marks corresponding to the pages of the 1516 edition. This was a manuscript of the widely used Byzantine version, familiar in the Greek Churches since the fourth century. Another text supplied by the Dominicans had the Byzantine text with a commentary by Theophylact to which Erasmus attached much importance. Reuchlin supplied another containing the whole of the New Testament except for the Apocalypse, and this too was from the twelfth century. As a more elegant, more easily read copy, it was used by Erasmus' assistants, Oecolampadius and Nikolaus Gerbel of Pfortzheim, in correcting the text during printing, but Erasmus considered it less trustworthy than the codex with Theophylact's commentary. For the Acts and Epistles he used yet another codex of the twelfth century which belonged to Johann Amerbach. Since none of these contained the Apocalypse he borrowed a further manuscript from Reuchlin that contained the Book of Revelation. This too was of the twelfth century, but the text was so closely interlined with the commentary that Erasmus had a clean copy made, and returned the original. In the course of making the copy, a number of errors were introduced which made their way into print. Moreover, the manuscript lacked the final leaf containing the last six verses of the text (22: 16–21). To supply the defect, Erasmus translated the missing verses from the Vulgate into Greek. Perhaps this is the best indication of the real importance Erasmus attached to the printing of the Greek New Testament. It was never meant to be a 'critical' text. The burden of his scholarship, and of what he wished to achieve, lay in the *Annotations*. Current scholarly opinion is summarized by M. A. Screech: 'Inside the volume the Greek original plays much the same role as the Annotations alone were originally intended to do: to justify the improvements and emendations to the Latin Vulgate.'

As for the Annotations, the 1516 edition incorporated the material collated during his stay in England, including some from early Latin manuscripts, two of them supplied by Colet. It may well have incorporated a residue from his abortive work on the Epistles of St Paul. His search for further manuscript authority was continued for the rest of his life, by visits to libraries, borrowing, and by consultation of the Aldine and Complutensian texts when these became available. Most of this new information went into successive editions of the *Annotations*, while the Greek text remained more or less unaltered after the first general revision of 1519. Moreover, it was less the Greek text that created a furore than the *Annotations*, where the Vulgate text is regularly challenged along with many of the scholastic authorities familiar to his readers. For the present, however, Erasmus sought the approval of Leo X to whom the *Novum instrumentum* was dedicated, and who obligingly wrote in 1518, to commend the forthcoming second edition (1519), 'go forward then in this same spirit: work for the public good, and do all you can to bring so religious an undertaking into the light of day, for you will receive from God himself a worthy reward for all your labours, from us the commendation you deserve, and from all Christ's faithful people lasting renown' (W 6.108).

If the *Novum instrumentum* is regarded as an attempt to produce a critical edition of the Greek New Testament, it will certainly add little to Erasmus' reputation as a textual scholar, especially when it is measured against the critical standards of a later age. But such an assessment fails to take into account Erasmus' real purpose, which was to introduce the literate community to a substantial revision of the Vulgate, supported by extensive annotations which were his main concern, and to show the same public the standard Greek text of the day for the enlightenment of the comparatively few who could read it. A recent scholar has commented that 'the Erasmus text is a typical Byzantine text and is the only sort of text conceivable two centuries before John Fell and John Mill'. In that respect at least the more carefully edited Complutensian Polyglot New Testament from Alcala was little different. That text had been printed already in 1514, and it is often surmised that Erasmus' Greek text was rushed into print in order to anticipate its publication. The Bible from Alcala was not published however until the entire work, including the Old Testament, had been printed and papal authorization obtained. It was finally released in 1522 in only 600 sets. For all of its peculiarities, seen through modern eyes, Froben's New Testament with Erasmus' name on its title-page sold some 3,000 copies in its first two editions.

There is little reason to doubt that it was the appeal of Erasmus' fresh and more elegant Latin version which guaranteed the work its popularity, along with the controversial and critical interest of the *Annotations*. Erasmus' Latin text of 1519 appears in the windows of King's College, Cambridge, an early and striking testimony to its instant popularity, and also to the influence of Richard Foxe, bishop of Winchester, who supervised the work on the windows. The text of 1519 was the basis of Luther's German translation, and through the third edition of Robert Estienne's Greek Testament (Paris, 1550), it heavily influenced the Greek Testament of Theodore Beza. It was Beza's text that underlay the King James version and the Elzevir Greek Testament in 1633, which proclaimed it the 'received text'. In this way was created the familiar *Textus receptus* for the New Testament, the foundation of biblical scholarship for three hundred years, until the era of 'higher criticism' began in the nineteenth century.

For Erasmus, however, the *Novum instrumentum* formed only a part, if a crucial one, in a continuing effort to revitalize the Christian life and understanding of Europe, and it is to that evangelism that we should now turn.

4 The philosophy of Christ

Erasmus' New Testament appeared with a remarkable, passionate prefatory piece. He called it *Paraclesis*—a Greek word meaning a summons or exhortation. It was that, and it was also a manifesto, the second of his life, matching the *Antibarbari*. In that first manifesto Erasmus had spelled out the reason for his devotion to the wisdom of pagan antiquity, as being a part of the divine plan, an instrument of God's self-revelation in his creation. The *Paraclesis* is an exhortation precisely to the universal mastery of that revelation as it was completed in Christ, the Word of God incarnate, the fullness of wisdom, discovered in scripture and appropriated as the rule of life. If the *Adagia* was the scholarly vindication and monument of that first manifesto, so the *Novum instrumentum* justified the second.

The *Paraclesis* used a term which was to become famous for its particular association with Erasmus, 'the philosophy of Christ'. It is easily misunderstood, and can be taken to indicate a rather rationalistic, moralizing attitude to Christianity, seeking to extract from it some general principles of conduct and, perhaps, the intimations of what might be called 'higher thought'. That was not what he intended. The term *philosophia Christi* is actually of patristic origin and its critical root is *sophia*—wisdom which is loved, and is of Christ. In that love there is the transforming power which Erasmus wishes to see affect the lives of men and women of all conditions, everywhere. They cannot love what they do not know, and what they seek (whether they know it or not) they will find in scripture. Why is it, he asks, that when men devote themselves so ardently to their studies, this study—the philosophy of Christ—is so neglected and derided, even by Christians? Since the enthusiasts of the many philosophical schools—Platonists, Pythagoreans, Stoics, and so forth—fight so fiercely for their convictions, 'why do we not evince far greater spirit for Christ, our Author and Prince?' (P 99). When we are initiated in his name by baptism, drawn to him by so many sacraments, why do we not think it

45

shameful to know nothing of his doctrines, which alone offer certain happiness? Moreover, mastery of this teaching is as nothing compared to the intricacies of such as Aristotle. 'The journey is simple, and it is ready for anyone. Only bring a pious and open mind, possessed above all with a pure and simple faith.' (P 100) The philosophy of Christ accommodates itself to the sophisticated as to the simple; 'not only does it serve the lowliest, but it is also an object of wonder to those at the top. . . . It is a small affair to the little ones and more than the highest affair to the great . . . . The sun itself is not as common and accessible to all as is Christ's teaching. It keeps no one at a distance, unless a person, begrudging himself, keeps himself away.' (P 101)

Erasmus further proclaims his conviction that scripture should even be made available in the common language of the people. 'Indeed, I disagree very much with those who are unwilling that Holy Scripture, translated into the vulgar tongue, be read by the uneducated, as if Christ taught such intricate doctrines that they could scarcely be understood by very few theologians, or as if the strength of the Christian religion consisted in men's ignorance of it . . . . I would that even the lowliest women read the Gospels and the Pauline Epistles. And I would that they were translated into all languages . . . '. Certainly, some will misunderstand, but some may be captivated. 'Would that, as a result, the farmer sing some portion of them at the plow, the weaver hum some parts of them to the movement of his shuttle, the traveler lighten the weariness of the journey with stories of this kind!' (P 101) This is the privilege, and the calling, of all. Since baptism is common in an equal degree to all Christians, and since the sacraments like the final reward of heaven are intended equally for all throughout their lives, why should the teachings of Christ be restricted to those who are called theologians and monks?

It is really sufficient to read the *Paraclesis* to grasp the heart of Erasmus' personal faith and concerns. All of the great issues are there: the universality of the Christian vocation, the enduring value of the great pagans, the dangers of formalism and mere ceremonialism, the damage done by the weakness and failures of the so-called professionals, the monks and theologians, the perverting of theology by those same professionals, who 'discuss earthly matters, not divine'—that is, who confuse and distort the Gospel of Christ by intricate syllogisms. The true theologian teaches 'by a disposition of mind, by his very expression and his eyes, by his very life'. And this vocation is open, not merely to the educated, but to the common labourer and the weaver. 'Another, perhaps even a non-Christian, may discuss more subtly how the angels understand'—an ironic thrust, surely—'but to persuade us here to lead an angelic life, free from every stain, this indeed is the duty of the Christian theologian' (P 102).

His concern was of course a familiar one—the interiorizing of conviction, 'meaning it'. What is needed for all the world is the peace and harmony that would spring up if we could see a generation of genuine Christians everywhere emerge, to 'restore the philosophy of Christ not in ceremonies alone and in syllogistic propositions but in the heart itself and in the whole life' (P 103). This is how Christendom's enemies should be conquered—by the allure of truth, manifested in the lives of those who profess to follow Christ. How, then, can anything be more important to us than 'the literature of Christ'? It is there that the philosophy of Christ is learned, located more truly in the disposition of the mind than in syllogisms, teaching that life means more than debate, inspiration is preferable to erudition, personal transformation to intellectual understanding. 'Only a very few can be learned, but all can be Christian, all can be devout, and—I shall boldly add—all can be theologians.' (P 104)

As if to anticipate an outcry at such a proclamation of lay authority, he insists that the philosophy of Christ has a special connaturality with human nature, so that it may easily penetrate into the minds of everyone. He picks up the thread of earlier argument by pointing to the analogy of pagan wisdom and virtue. 'What else is the philosophy of Christ, which he himself calls a rebirth, than the restoration of human nature originally well formed?' (P 104) Thus we find in the books of the pagans much that agrees with Christ's teaching: the Stoics, the Platonic Socrates, Aristotle in his *Politics*, and even Epicurus, are all called to witness to such parallels. Yet all of this wisdom is most fully realized in the teaching of Christ, who should

47

come first among all teachers of the past. Yet knowledge of his doctrine is not enough; it is essential also to carry it into effect. Here is the thrust of his objection to the 'modern' theologians. 'Not that I condemn the industry of those who not without merit employ their native intellectual powers in such subtle discourse, for I do not wish anyone to be offended, but that I think . . . that the pure and genuine philosophy of Christ is not to be drawn from any source more abundantly than from the evangelical books and from the apostolic letters, about which, if anyone should devoutly philosophize, praying more than arguing and seeking to be transformed rather than armed for battle, he would without a doubt find that there is nothing pertaining to the happiness of man and the living of his life which is not taught, examined, and unraveled in these works.' In truth, in the pages of scripture we meet the living, breathing Christ himself, 'I should say almost more effectively than when He dwelt among men. The Jews saw and heard less than you see and hear in the books of the Gospels . . .' (P 105).

Erasmus then points with dismay to the fact that while both Jews and Muslims study and venerate their scriptures from childhood on, Christians will study, seemingly, almost any other author first: authors of religious rules (he does not exempt the Augustinians), authors of the theological canon—Albertus Magnus, Aquinas, Giles of Viterbo, Richard of St Victor, William of Occam—while they neglect the writings which alone are attested by God himself. While acknowledging the merits and efforts of such writers, Erasmus is ever conscious of the wrangles and disputes which divide the various schools of theology and their adherents. In a final and moving plea for Christian nurture in the teachings of scripture he urges, 'let earliest childhood be formed by the Gospels of him whom I would wish particularly presented in such a way that children also might love him' (P 107). He should in time form every child to full maturity; he should be the consolation of all at the end of life. How much more deserving of our devotion even than the relics of sanctity are the pages of scripture where we find the 'living and breathing likeness'. 'We embellish a wooden or stone statue with gems and gold for the love of Christ. Why not, rather, mark with gold and gems and with ornaments of greater value than these, if such there be, these writings which bring Christ to us so much more effectively than any paltry image? The latter represents only the form of the body—if indeed it represents anything of him—but these writings bring you the living image of his holy mind and the speaking, healing, dying, rising Christ himself, and thus they render him so fully present that you would see less if you gazed upon him with your very eyes.' (P 108)

The *Paraclesis* appeared in 1516 with the first version of Erasmus' New Testament. Two and a half years later, in August 1518, there appeared another preface which confirmed his view that Christian understanding must find its fruit in a life of personal piety, and that this is the first and essential task before every Christian. This was the letter to Paul Volz, a Benedictine abbot, introducing a new edition of the *Enchiridion militis Christiani*. The *Enchiridion*, or *Handbook of the Christian Soldier*, was written, as we noted, at the time Erasmus became acquainted with Jean Vitrier and, through him, acquainted also with the works of Origen. It was first printed in Antwerp in 1503, coincidentally the very year that Volz had first taken on the life of a monk. Erasmus had come to know Volz as a member of the literary circle in Schlettstadt (Sélestat), and Volz's interest in reforming his monastic community at Hugshofen may have reminded Erasmus of Vitrier. At any rate, while the first edition of the *Enchiridion* had attracted little attention, the new edition by Froben ushered in an era when it became one of the most widely read and often translated spiritual writings of the age. Vernacular translations, almost invariably including the prefatory letter to Volz, appeared in print in Czech (1519), German (1520), Dutch (1523), Spanish (1525), French (1529), Italian (1531), English (1533), Polish (1558), Swedish (1592), Hungarian (1627), and Russian (1783). It remained Erasmus' most influential single statement about the life of piety, and by implication, about the nature of theology and even of the Christian Church.

Despite the evidence for the remarkable impact of the *Enchiridion* on the public of Christendom—Marcel Bataillon for example revealed its popularity in Spain, where the translation was reprinted twelve times before 1556—a modern reader may find it difficult to recognize in it a work of almost revolutionary import. In order to grasp its significance we must know something of the background. A brief digression here will lead us to a better understanding of Erasmus' personal mission.

The background is the immense, sophisticated, and magisterial enterprise of scholastic theology—the theology of the 'Schools'. In the twelfth and thirteenth centuries, with the reception of Aristotle in the West and the growth of university teaching, theology began to take on the nature of a professional discipline. In place of the long-established method of a reflective reading of scripture and the Fathers following the manner of the ancient rhetorical disciplines, and structured by the liturgical cycle of the Church, there emerged the ideal of a coherent, rational system, formed by the categories of Aristotelian logic. By the middle of the thirteenth century Aristotelian rationalism had conquered the Faculty of Arts at Paris completely, and it posed an immense challenge to the traditional intellectual habits of Christendom.

In the vast synthesis of Aquinas, theology, while primarily speculative, also dealt importantly with the practical, moral life. The largest section of the *Summa theologiae*—the *Secunda pars*—was entirely concerned with this. Erasmus knew it and, seemingly, had little quarrel with its teaching. Its sheer bulk and technical organization, however, made it the preserve of the initiates, the academic theologians. Later developments of the fourteenth century led further in the direction of speculative theology and away from the Bible and the Fathers, so that the earlier view of Christian life in the Spirit as an integral whole receded. Although the earlier methods of studying the sacred page continued in the monasteries and within certain other centres, the 'new theology' associated with the names of Scotus and Occam carried the day: it was academic, rationalistic, and speculative. Those looking to theology for spiritual sustenance and practical guidance were left hungry; some, like Jean Gerson, began to develop a 'mystical theology' over against the theology of the Schools, increasingly dominated by endless disputes and subtle argumentation. These debates were to provide a wealth of illustration for Erasmus' satirical attacks. One consequence of these developments was the civil warfare among the learned which Erasmus decried as futile in principle, and, what was worse, perilous to Christian unity. A second consequence was the practical divorce of preaching and devotion among the ordinary clergy and laity from the sophisticated distractions of the academic theologians.

In their work as such it is fair to say that Erasmus took little interest. For this he paid a price, as he found in his controversy with Luther (among others). His constant preoccupation was with the calling of all the baptized to the fullness of a life lived wholly in the love of Christ. In that life of piety—*pietas*—the speculations of the intellect had, to be sure, a legitimate place, as he would occasionally admit. So did concern with right doctrine, good morals, contemplative prayer, the service of others, and, in all things, the effective preaching of the Good News by a life well-lived. This was a seamless fabric, where different gifts called forth different missions from the baptized. But no undertaking, however worthy in itself, might be allowed to obscure the message of Christ. Erasmus thus admits to Volz that his little book says nothing about Scotistic problems. 'Penetration I can do without, provided there is piety. It need not equip men for the wrestling-schools of the Sorbonne if it equips them for the tranquillity proper to a Christian. It need not contribute to theological discussion provided it contributes to the life that befits a theologian.' (V 8)

The *Enchiridion* then was meant to supply an epitome of doctrine and exhortation combined, to instruct and inspire its reader in the life of true piety. 'Who can carry the *Secunda secundae* of Aquinas round with him? And yet the good life is everybody's business, and Christ wished the way to it to be accessible to all men, not beset with impenetrable labyrinths of argument, but open to sincere faith, to love unfeigned, and to their companion, the hope that is not put to shame.' By all means let eminent professionals pore over the great tomes of theological science. None the less, 'we must take thought all the time for the unlettered multitude for whom Christ died' (V 9).

It follows also that the *Enchiridion* was not meant to be a handbook of meditation like the *Imitation of Christ* to which it is sometimes compared, unfavourably. Erasmus' aim was educational, as always. It was most simply stated in the first sentence of his original dedication: to set down 'a kind of summary guide to living, so that, equipped with it, you might attain to a state of mind worthy of Christ' (E 24). As a work both of instruction and exhortation, acquainting its reader with the essentials of the Christian faith secured by 'the sheet-anchor of Gospel teaching' and inciting as well to a love of him who is the source of that teaching, it was an effective summary of the *philosophia Christi*.

The work was dedicated to a worldly layman, possibly a successful gunsmith of Mechelen named Poppenruyter, whose family was known to Erasmus. The metaphor of the Christian soldier had an ironic relevance, therefore, but it was taken of course from St Paul, whose imagery pervades the work and whose epistles provide most of the scriptural citations. Life is a warfare waged, on the one hand, against the forces of vice without and, within, against the 'old, earthly Adam'. It is our habit to ignore our true predicament and, 'as if our life were not warfare, but a Greek symposium, we roll around in our beds . . . We are garlanded with roses and the delights of Adonis rather than girded in harsh armour.' (E 25) At baptism, however, all were enrolled in the army of Christ, our general, to whom we owe our lives. We have pledged our loyalty to him. The prize of loyal service under Christ's banner is blessed immortality. We must seek it, since the worst the enemy can do is to destroy our earthly bodies, which we shall one day lose to death anyway. The supreme disaster is the death of the soul.

The Christian should prepare for service, then, by putting on the armour of the Christian militia. Two weapons in particular are important: prayer and knowledge. Prayer binds us to the goal of heaven, and knowledge fortifies the intellect with salutary opinions; each complements and guides the other. A fervent study of the scriptures is essential both to prayer and the acquisition of essential knowledge. Moreover, Erasmus does not hesitate to recommend 'a kind of preliminary training' in the pagan poets and philosophers, provided such studies are pursued with moderation and at the right stage. Basil, Augustine, Jerome, and Cyprian are all invoked in support of this opinion. While he would not want the Christian soldier to imbibe pagan morals,

the pagans can instruct us well in many things which are conducive to a holy life. 'These writings shape and invigorate the
child's mind and provide an admirable preparation for the
understanding of the divine Scriptures, for it is almost an act of
sacrilege to rush into these studies without due preparation.'
Erasmus' rooted conviction about the interrelatedness of pagan
and Christian wisdom is thus proclaimed at the very outset of
the *Enchiridion*. He recommends in particular the poetry of
Homer and Virgil, provided the reader remembers that their
poetry is entirely allegorical ('no one who has had even the
slightest acquaintance with ancient learning will deny this'), a
rule to bear in mind in reading scripture as well. The 'obscene
poets' are to be avoided. Of the philosophers, he recommends
the Platonists 'because in much of their thinking as well as in
their mode of expression they are the closest to the spirit of the
prophets and of the gospel'. There would be profit, indeed, in a
taste of all pagan literature, if it is taken at the appropriate time
and with moderation, caution, and discrimination, 'more in the
manner of a foreign visitor than a resident, and lastly and most
important, if it all be related to Christ' (E 33).

At its best, however, the learning of the great pagans will be
'unleavened bread', temporary nourishment which will not do
for the long journey. For that the Christian soldier will need the
manna of heavenly wisdom, found only in the sacred scriptures.
These must be approached only with great purity of mind.
Regard them as nothing less than oracles. 'You will feel that you
are inspired, moved, swept away, transfigured in an ineffable
manner by the divine power if you approach them with respect,
veneration, and humility.' (E 34) The best interpreters of scripture are those who depart as much as possible from the literal
sense. Paul is first, then Origen, Ambrose, Jerome, and
Augustine. 'I notice', he remarks, 'that modern theologians are
too willing to stick to the letter and give their attention to
sophistic subtleties rather than to the elucidation of the
mysteries, as if Paul were not right in saying that our law is
spiritual.' And he goes on, 'If you prefer to be strong spiritually
rather than clever in debate, if you seek sustenance for the soul
rather than mere titillation of the intellect, read and reread the
ancient commentators in preference to all others, since their

piety is more proven, their learning more profuse and more experienced, their style neither jejune nor impoverished, and their interpretation more fitted to the sacred mysteries. I do not say this because I look down upon the moderns, but because I prefer writings that are more useful and more conducive to your purpose.' (E 35)

Erasmus' concern to avoid the letter for the spirit reflects his constant preoccupation with the interior, spiritual reality. In this instance he urges the reader to care and patience in approaching scripture, where knowledgeable meditation on a single verse can provide more spiritual nourishment than 'the whole Psalter chanted monotonously with regard only for the letter'. He witnesses to this from his own experience as a failing both of the common people and of the religious professionals. 'I think the principal reason why we see that monastic piety is everywhere so cold, languid, and almost extinct is that they are growing old in the letter and never take pains to learn the spiritual sense of the scriptures. They do not hear Christ crying out in the gospel: "The flesh is of no profit; it is the spirit that gives life".' (E 35)

The object of all this endeavour is the true wisdom which teaches us how to live. That true wisdom is found only in Christ its author, who is, indeed, wisdom itself. He is the light that banishes darkness, reflection of the glory of the Father who, 'as he became redemption and justification to us who were reborn in him according to the testimony of Paul, so he also became wisdom'. This wisdom has nothing to do with the self-styled wisdom of this world, whose end is perdition, 'because pernicious arrogance always follows after it as its attendant, arrogance is then followed by blindness of spirit, blindness by the tyranny of the emotions, and this by a whole harvest of vices and the freedom to commit every manner of sin' (E 40).

How then, do we attain to the wisdom of Christ? The beginning is to achieve self-knowledge, says Erasmus, citing one of the first of his Adages. All antiquity believed that this saying came down from heaven, but it would have little authority with us if it did not also accord with scripture. Such knowledge is not easy. Even the great Paul, who was raised to see the mysteries of the third heaven, did not presume to judge himself since he knew himself insufficiently. What self-assurance then, can ordinary creatures have? In order to assist, Erasmus now presents his reader with a likeness of human nature, 'as in a painting, so that you may have a clear knowledge of what you are on the inside and what you are skin-deep' (E 41).

There follows an anthropology which underlies all of Erasmus' thought on religion and moral duty. It is based on St Paul seen especially through the eyes of Origen, and reflects strongly the generalized influence of Plato. We have noticed already Erasmus' respect for the philosophy of Plato as being particularly congenial to the Christian outlook, but he was much less syncretic than were many of the Neoplatonic disciples of the Renaissance. Where Ficino and others drew enthusiastically and eclectically on the theories of pagan Neoplatonists such as Plotinus, Erasmus' sensitivity to the early centuries of Christianity, and to the nuances of the Christological controversies, prevented his wandering too far into the world of Philo of Alexandria or the Pseudo-Dionysius. His discrimination was probably reinforced by firm disposition towards the practical, and his dislike of any hint of teaching reserved for the initiates—hermeticism and the Cabbala were never to his taste. His Platonism came directly from Plato himself, and, indirectly, from the influence of such Fathers as those he recommends in the *Enchiridion*.

This influence is clear at the next stage of his *Handbook*, where Erasmus describes the respective claims of the inner and the outer man. Self-knowledge, it seems, is chiefly awareness of the conflict between the inward and outer natures. Erasmus' platonizing tendencies lead him consistently to imply that the body as such restrains the aspirations of man's higher nature. There is here a genuine confusion, at times, between St Paul's 'flesh' and the Platonic body, which is gross in nature and an obstacle intrinsically to the destiny of the soul. However, the Pauline 'flesh' denoted not the physical body but the entirety of the unredeemed nature, and it is sufficiently clear that no notion of the body as intrinsically evil or sinful could be reconciled with the central Christian doctrine of the incarnation. Such confusion none the less occurred among many Christian writers through the ages, as it does also in Erasmus.

Erasmus' view of the intrinsic antipathy of body and soul is apparent from the outset, when he states that man is composed of 'a soul which is like a divinity and a body which is like a brute beast'. Our bodies indeed are inferior to those of the beasts, while our souls have such a capacity for divinity 'that we can soar past the minds of the angels and become one with God'. At one time united in harmony by their Creator, these two natures have remained in unhappy discord since the Fall, so that each with regard to the other 'holds the wolf by the ears' (E 41). The mortal body pursues temporal things and sinks downward; the soul, 'remembering its heavenly origin', pursues the spiritual and imperishable, and struggles upwards against the weight of its earthly burden. Before sin broke the primal harmony of all creation, our reason commanded the body without difficulty; now, the passions strive to take reason captive. In a vaguely Platonic analogy between human nature and a turbulent republic, Erasmus likens the reason to the supreme ruler, certain worthy emotions (filial respect, love of family and friends, desire for good reputation) to the nobles, and the base passions (lust, envy, debauchery) to the 'lowest dregs of the masses' (E 42). Plato's understanding of this state of affairs Erasmus attributes to divine inspiration, since 'the authority of the philosophers would be of little effect if all those same teachings were not contained in the sacred scriptures, even if not in the same words' (E 47). What the philosophers call reason, Erasmus states, Paul calls either spirit or the inner man or the law of the mind; what they call passions he calls the flesh, the body, the outer man, or the law. While these explanations may leave one uneasy, Erasmus does not forget to acknowledge some role for divine grace, although not by that name. He states that in mastering the base passions we cannot rely upon our own strength, 'but if you have recourse to God as your helper, nothing is easier' (E 46). St Paul instructs us: when troubled by vice we must implore divine assistance immediately by repeated prayers.

To amplify these lessons and drive them home, Erasmus turns explicitly to Origen concerning St Paul's tripartite division of human nature: spirit, soul, and flesh. The body (the flesh) is the lowest part, carrier of the sin of our first parents, through which we are incited to evil; the spirit is that in which we resemble the divine author of our being, where 'the supreme maker has engraved with his finger, that is his Spirit, the eternal law of goodness, drawn from the archetype of his own mind' (E 51), and through this we are joined to God; finally, the 'middle soul' is capable of sensations and natural movements. The soul is buffeted, free to incline to one side or the other. Thus the spirit makes us gods, the flesh brute animals, and the presence of the soul constitutes us as human beings. 'Natural' virtues are the realm of the soul: love of parents and children, loyalty to friends—the pagans do as much. But if these dispositions come into conflict with a higher law, requiring us to neglect our duties to a parent, to override affection for our children or a friend, our soul is at a crossroads, solicited by the flesh on the one side, by the spirit on the other. 'The spirit says, "God is to be preferred to one's parent. To the latter you owe merely your body, to God you owe everything." The flesh suggests: "If you do not obey, your father will disinherit you, and people will say that you have no respect for your father. Be practical, think of your reputation." ' (E 52)

Erasmus urges the Christian soldier to accustom himself to this mode of 'shrewd self-examination'. It is easy to think that a natural instinct is perfect piety, and Erasmus points out that personalities differ widely in their natural tastes and endowments. Some are little tempted by the pleasures of the flesh; they should beware of attributing to virtue something in itself indifferent. Others find pleasure in fasting, or in church attendance. In each case we must ask where their inclinations lie, and what they seek by what they do. If it is public reputation, then these actions smack not of the spirit, but of the flesh. 'A brother has need of your help, but you mumble your miserable little prayers to God while ignoring the need of your brother. God will not be favourable to your prayers. How will God hear your prayers when you do not hear your fellow man?' (E 53) A second example touches on marriage. A man may love his wife simply because she is his wife; the pagans do as much. Or love her because she gives him pleasure; then the love is carnal. 'But', continues Erasmus, 'if you love her above all because you perceive in her the image of Christ, for example, piety, modesty, sobriety, and chastity, and you no longer love her in herself but in Christ, or rather Christ in her, then your love is spiritual.' (E 53–4)

With this as a framework for self-examination, Erasmus turns now to some practical rules to be used 'as if they were wrestling holds' in coping with the errors of the world and attaining the pure light of the spiritual life. They will be effective especially against three evils which are vestiges of original sin, for 'even if baptism has removed the stain, nevertheless a residue of the old malady remains in us both as a safeguard of humility and as a raw material and a fertile terrain for virtue' (E 54). These three evils are blindness, the flesh, and weakness. Blindness impairs judgement, the flesh corrupts the will, and weakness destroys constancy. To avoid these evils, we must know how to distinguish between things to be avoided and those to be sought; we must hate evil once it is recognized and love good; finally, we must persevere in our undertakings for good and virtuous causes.

The twenty-one 'rules of combat' which follow vary widely in length of treatment. The Christian soldier is urged to inform himself thoroughly about the Christ whom he follows from scripture, and to believe what he learns there with his whole heart. He must be resolute in his purpose, aware that he cannot serve two masters. He must keep in view the nature of his reward, against the illusory rewards of this world. Christ should be kept before him at all times as his only goal, and all neutral goods and undertakings should be weighed solely for their use in acquiring virtue. There is an interesting personal illustration in the fourth rule drawn from the love of letters, a neutral thing in itself. It is worthy if letters are pursued for the sake of Christ, not if the possession of knowledge alone gives pleasure. 'If you have confidence in yourself and hope for an immense reward in Christ, continue on your way like a bold merchant, ranging afar in the realms of pagan letters, and convert the riches of Egypt into the adornment of the Lord's temple. But if you fear a greater loss than gain, return to the first rule, know yourself, and measure yourself by your own standard. It is better to know less and love more than to know more and not love.' (E 62)

The fifth and sixth rules deal with piety as a passage from

visible to invisible goods, and with Christ as the sole archetype of the Christian. Together, they allow Erasmus to range through a variety of topics and rehearse many of his favourite themes, and, in the same way, they anticipate many passages in the *Praise of Folly*. The reader is urged under rule five to learn the value of allegory in pagan wisdom as in scripture, as a clue to the inner meaning of life. One such teaches the importance of following our natural inclinations provided they are morally acceptable; thus, 'do not entangle yourself in marriage if celibacy is more suitable to your character, and conversely, do not vow yourself to celibacy if you seem more adapted to the married state, for whatever you attempt against your natural inclination usually turns out to be unsuccessful' (E 68).

In remembering the importance of the mystery underlying the form, Erasmus gives the example of the daily celebration of mass. If this is done while living for oneself and heedless of the fortunes of one's neighbours, then the celebrant is still in the 'flesh' of the sacrament. 'But if in offering sacrifice you are conscious of the meaning of that partaking, namely, that you are one spirit with the spirit of Christ, one body with the body of Christ, a living member of the church, if you love nothing but in Christ, if you consider all your goods to be the common property of all men, if you are afflicted by the misfortunes of others as if they were your own, then you celebrate mass with great profit, since you do so spiritually.' (E 71)

The practical import of Erasmus' 'rules' is shown in the illustrations, and they are aimed clearly at those in ordinary circumstances of life, lay or clerical. We are to live only for God as members of one body, to aim at the best and, at the very least, refrain from base conduct; we cannot allow ourselves to be discouraged by temptations or failures; we must be vigilant at all times, most of all when we feel that we are succeeding. We should arm ourselves with passages of scripture against temptation, and beware of spiritual pride. In repudiating sin, we must press beyond the victory to an extra assertion of penance or further virtue. View each battle as the last, but remain alert to the danger of false, *self*-confidence. No vice is negligible; be complacent about none. When we are daunted by the task of resisting sin, we should remember the painful burden that surrender will impose.

These and like counsels are intended not to inspire immediately, but to show the aspirant how to discipline his imagination by the acquisition of knowledge and effective habits; when viewed in this light, it is less surprising that the *Enchiridion* has been seen as the basis for many of the spiritual manuals and methods (like the Ignatian *Exercises*) that followed in the next generation. Erasmus concludes with an Epilogue of remedies (E 117) against certain of the more common sins: lust, avarice, ambition ('the only honour to be sought after by a Christian is to be praised not by men, but by God'), haughtiness and arrogance of mind, anger and the desire for revenge. In these 'epilogues' there is much down-to-earth, pastoral advice to drive home the more wide-ranging precepts before. Erasmus takes his leave by pointing out what a 'vast sea of vices' still remains to be discussed, and gives these over to the resourcefulness of his reader following the method and rule already supplied. Against all vices the mind must be fortified well in advance of their attack, 'by prayer, the sayings of wise men, the doctrines of scripture, the example of pious men and especially of Christ'. Finally, the reader is exhorted to associate with those only in whom he has seen Christ's true image, and to make Paul his special friend—to be kept in his pocket and committed to memory.

What we find in the *Enchiridion* is authentically a fresh vision of the Christian life for contemporary Europeans. It was not an adapted form of monastic spirituality, like the English devotion or the *Devotio moderna* of the previous century, which had recruited followers into separate communities and something like a regular life. However important those movements proved to be, they can be seen as attempts to refurbish accepted ideals, to reassert old standards, or to broaden the base of established forms by adapting them to a laity eager for a richer spiritual life than the conventions of common worship made available.

The vision of the *Enchiridion* is of a Christian society in which the mode of life adopted is entirely secondary to the personal commitment of each of the baptized to perfection in Christ. No special prestige is attached to the clerical state, or to vows of consecrated life—these are worthy provided they are appropriate to the individuals concerned and are lived with complete integrity. Equally valid, by implication, is the vocation of those married and living 'in the world', and their charter of citizenship within the Christian polity, so to speak, is placed in the foreground with the warm reception of pagan literature both as an introduction to scripture and as a valid source of practical, ethical wisdom. Particularly evident is the lack of deference to clerical direction: each follower of this handbook is meant to be equipped as his own spiritual director, under Christ. This was a radical departure indeed—more radical, perhaps, than its author intended.

Something of Erasmus' general vision can be gathered from the most remarkable passage in the letter to Volz with which this discussion opened. This is a portrait of the Church which is original with him, and which appeared also in his important treatise on theological method, the *Ratio verae theologiae* in the same year, 1518. Here the Christian community is pictured as ranged in three concentric circles, focusing like the rings of a target on the person of Christ. (E 14) In the innermost circle, nearest to Christ, are the priests, bishops, cardinals, and popes, and 'all whose duty is to follow the Lamb wherever he shall go'. These must embrace the intense purity of the centre and pass on as much as they can to those next to them. Their neighbours in the second circle are the secular princes, whose arms and laws must be devoted to Christ's service in just war, defence of public peace, or in restraint of evil-doers through lawful punishment. Their contribution to the true ends of a Christian society then is essentially restorative: the danger is that they may turn their power to their private advantage instead of the public good. It is a prime responsibility of the members of the priestly order to call them to their duties.

In the third circle are the common people, the 'most earthy portion of this world, but not so earthy that they are not members of Christ's body just the same' (E 15). They must be nourished and encouraged, since each according to the measure that is given him must strive upwards towards Christ. Erasmus then adds as an afterthought, 'If now someone thinks that this circle is more suitable for princes, there will be no serious difference of opinion between us. For if we observe their characters, we shall hardly find Christians more rudimentary than they.' (E 16)

Outside this third circle is everything abominable: ambition, love of money, lechery, anger, revenge, and the like. These are dangerous when they disguise themselves under the mask of religion and duty, as when tyrannical power is used under a pretext of justice and right. What must be impressed upon all is that the one goal of life is Christ and his teaching in all its purity. Since the perfection of Christ is in the interior dispositions, not in the external mode of life, Erasmus makes it clear that the places people occupy in the various circles as they appear to one another do not necessarily reflect the true, invisible relationship of the members with respect to Christ.

Even on the face of it, this is a remarkable image indeed. Erasmus sees the Christian commonwealth as a polity of the baptized without elaborate institutional structure. It centres on Christ, and worldly rank within it is justified only by responsibility—the special duties of the clergy, the corresponding duties of the princes. There is also an invisible ranking, known only to God, defined by the holiness of the members. In this spiritual commonwealth, some of those in the inner circle are at the furthest remove from the centre, while some of those who are most humble in worldly terms are most exalted in their true nearness to Christ. Much could be said and more conjectured about the nuances and implications of this image. For the political and social radicalism latent within it, to comment no further, we are bound to recall Erasmus' situation when the *Enchiridion* was first written, and the radical Franciscan spiritualism to which his then host, Jean Vitrier, was heir. We must recall as well that a large part of his time and energy in the years especially after 1515 was spent in unsparing criticism of the religion, politics, and morals of his day, and in running combat with controversialists who rose on every side. It was an ironic fate for one whose professed ideals were irenicism and concord.

5 The problem of Luther

Without question, Erasmus could be infuriating. His high ideals for the reformation and renewal of Christendom—not simply, 'the Church'—could be advanced with moving sincerity and evident conviction. Almost as frequently, however, they were proposed in a way calculated to arouse the mirth of many, the ire of some, and the enmity of not a few. He invited this response in part by the use of one of his most formidable literary weapons, the coruscating satire of which he was the greatest exponent since his own master, Lucian, the first-century rhetorician of Samosata. The frustration and suspicion of his critics was provoked also by their lack of familiarity and sympathy with his humanist intellectual culture, so alien to their own. This was true not only of contemporary defenders of tradition but also of the followers of the prophetic figure who emerged as Erasmus' rival and nemesis, Martin Luther.

Erasmus' use of satire, congenial as it was to his nature, had a deeply serious intent. He beguiled his readers into examination of their accepted notions, not by challenging them directly, but by exposing contradictions and absurdities, and by the subtle flattery of presuming the harmony of their superior judgement with his own. Vulgar pieties, prelatic pride, kingly vanity, and common greed, indolence, imposture, credulity, and deceit, all were haled into the light of Lucianic wit and reason. Behind the play of irony and wit the claims of the philosophy of Christ were advanced relentlessly against the entire apparatus of religious conventions which, in his judgement, too often distracted the well-intentioned faithful from the one thing necessary—the personal claim upon their lives of 'the speaking, healing, dying, rising Christ himself' (P 108).

In order to provoke his readers to think about their religion anew he risked misunderstanding and scandal. Wittingly or not, he became a master of disenchantment, and the gibes in his *Colloquies* and elsewhere in his voluminous works could be judged with reason to have prepared the way, for many, for that great recasting of belief which became Protestant Christianity. An early convert in England, an Austin Friar who was tried by Tunstall in 1528, traced the beginnings of his apostasy from the Catholic faith to the influence of Erasmus. 'All Christian men beware of consenting to Erasmus' Fables,' he testified, 'for by consenting to them they have caused me to shrink in my faith, that I promised to God at my christening by my witnesses.' He cited the influence of the 'Colloquium' in particular, and concluded sadly, 'Thus I mused of these opinions so greatly, that my mind was almost withdrawn from devotion to saints. Notwithstanding, I consented that the divine service of them was very good and is, though I have not had such sweetness in it as I should have had because of such fables.'

Since it is perfectly clear that Erasmus approved of traditional devotions properly understood and said so repeatedly, and equally evident that his whole purpose was to increase true devotion rather than to diminish it, we are drawn to conclude that here, as with his New Testament, he failed to appreciate the potential impact of notions familiar to his learned intimates once they were disseminated in print and by translations.

Among his learned contemporaries outside the humanist community, there was little understanding of the intellectual basis of his views or of his criticisms. An important and exemplary episode concerns his rendering of the famous opening of the Gospel of St John, 'In the beginning was the Word', by translating 'Word' with the Latin *sermo* in place of the Vulgate's *verbum*. The change was made in the second edition of his New Testament (1519), and the decision was rooted in convictions about the creative power of the Word which we have discussed already. His new Latin rendering of the Greek *logos* might be translated (if imprecisely): 'In the beginning there was Speech; that Speech was in the beginning with God, and everything God made, he made by speaking' (cf. Bo 3). It altered the conception of Word from a static entity to an active presence, and it reveals a fundamental principle of Erasmus' outlook, that the divine *logos*, incarnate in Christ, continues through all of time to instruct God's people and to sustain and inform all of creation. In this conception, Christ as *sermo* incarnate was nothing less than the very eloquence of God, more vivid, more vital and present than any concept, any mere *verbum* or 'word'. In the *Ecclesiastes*, his great treatise on preaching, Erasmus refers to Christ as *sermo Dei*—the 'discourse of God'—and goes on thus: 'Through this (*sermo Dei*) the Father established the universe, through this he governs everything he established, through this he restored the fallen human family, through this he binds the Church to himself.' (Mc 84)

There was a storm of controversy. It was led by an English friar, Henry Standish, an Oxford graduate and popular preacher at court, who was provincial of the English Franciscans until 1518, when he had been appointed bishop of St Asaph's. Standish was a well-regarded professional in theology. He saw in the change not merely a philological decision but a theological meaning. In fact it was a philological decision, but it had implications of the second kind. Ill equipped as a philologist, Standish fell back upon the argument that this term violated the sacred text and was unprecedented. He was horribly wrong. Erasmus argued easily that *sermo* and *verbum* were used interchangeably in the Bible as well as patristic writing to denote the Son of God. Thomas More came to his defence both at the English court and in print, pointing to the precedents in tradition, especially in patristic commentators, noting that Gregory of Nazianzus said the Son of God was called *logos*, 'not only because he is Speech and the Word but also because he is Reason and Wisdom', and adding that, in his own view, the word might well be kept in its original form, like 'Alleluia', 'Kyrie eleison', 'Amen', and 'Osanna'.

Here was an exemplary instance of the kind of disagreement that could arise from divergence between humanistic and traditional, scholastic culture. It would be gratifying to report that Erasmus, the devoted teacher, used the opportunity to convert Standish to his own way of thinking. Nothing could be further from the truth. Much as he taught the importance of persuasion, Erasmus almost never applied his own principles in exchanges with his critics—quite the contrary. He bristled with indignation and flew to the attack. He had had Standish in his sights for some time as a suspected critic of his edition of Jerome, and named him in 1517 among theologians who rule the roost under 'some black theological planet'. He now accused Standish and his allies of ignorance, malice, and ingratitude; they were 'unfair', 'shameless', 'brainless', 'sycophants'. They were added to the growing number chiefly in the religious orders whom Erasmus saw as something close to an organized conspiracy to defame the cause of good letters in general, and Erasmus in particular. Since it was a time when public vituperation perhaps reached its apogee, it is difficult to make a final judgement, but it is clear enough that Erasmus' conduct of controversy did nothing to diminish the number of his detractors, nor to add to those converted to his way of thinking.

The Standish affair serves to illustrate a myriad of controversies which absorbed an increasing portion of Erasmus' time and energy after 1515. Inevitably the more he wrote, the more he invited criticism and attack, until polemics came to dominate his literary output. In the catalogue of works he drew up in 1523 for Johann von Botzheim he wrote, 'The eighth volume will contain the apologies. And—how sad for me!—they will make up a complete volume.' (W 9.355) None of those controversies could approach in historic importance the one which was now awaiting him, the debate with Martin Luther.

There was a generation between them; Luther could almost have been Erasmus' son. Born in November 1483, he was a young Augustinian professor at Wittenberg in the very years when Erasmus was emerging as the foremost humanist in northern Europe, as a pioneering editor of the Fathers and of the New Testament, as a master of the literary tradition and a brilliant critic of contemporary society. Like so many, Luther was Erasmus' pupil, in part. He turned to his writings for an understanding of the New Testament, for the edition of Jerome, for the *Adages*, *Praise of Folly*, and works of devotion. In many ways they shared concerns about the Church, though not about the place of antiquity in education. Both rejected the supremacy of Aristotle and the system of the Schoolmen, both proclaimed the central place of the Bible in Christian life, emphasized the perils of religious formalism, denounced the abuse of indulgences, and urged the princes to take the reform of the Church in hand. The religion of the *Enchiridion* and the *Paraclesis* was common to them both. However beneath such surface agreement, which was shared after all with many others, there lay widely differing temperaments and priorities.

As early as 1516 Luther remarked, 'In the exposition of the Scripture I put Jerome as far behind Augustine as Erasmus puts Augustine behind Jerome.' A letter of the next year reveals that Luther's preoccupations were beginning to detach him from Erasmus: 'I am at present reading our Erasmus, but my mind is moving more and more away from him . . . I fear he does not spread Christ and God's grace sufficiently abroad . . . the human is of more importance to him than the divine.' (Ru 264)

For his part, Erasmus showed an immediate sympathy with the aims of the young Luther when he first encountered them. Luther had learned from friends that Erasmus admired his theses on indulgences and had seen his sympathy confirmed in the letter to Paul Volz which prefaced the 1518 edition of the *Enchiridion*. Encouraged, he evidently overcame his misgivings and reached out to the older man, acknowledging in a letter of March 1519 'that wonderful spirit of yours which has so much enriched me and all of us'. 'Though you know it not,' Luther continued, 'I possess your spirit and all that you do for us in your books, without exchange of letters or converse with you in person. . . . And so, dear Erasmus, kindest of men, if you see no objection, accept this younger brother of yours in Christ, who is at least much devoted to you and full of affection . . .' (W 6.282).

Erasmus' reply from Louvain (May 1519) is a study in rhetorical skill, since he managed almost in the same breath to extend his friendship and distance himself from Luther. Greeting Luther as 'dearest brother in Christ' and thanking him for his letter, Erasmus at once remarked on the storm raised by his books. 'Even now it is impossible to root out from men's minds the most groundless suspicion that your work is written with assistance from me and that I am, as they call it, a standard-bearer of this new movement.' Erasmus feared with reason that their alleged association would give the enemies of humane letters a new reason to oppose them, 'as likely to stand in the way of her majesty, queen Theology, whom they value much more than they do Christ. . . . In the whole business their weapons are clamour, audacity, subterfuge, misinterpretation, innuendo; if I had not seen it with my own eyes—felt it, rather—I would never have believed theologians could be such maniacs!

One would think it was some disastrous infection . . .'
(W 6.391). By this stage in the letter Erasmus had become
wholly preoccupied with his personal situation in the university, but the main points of his public defence of Luther were
clearly stated: Luther's opponents should do him the courtesy of
reading what he has written; and it would behove them to discuss his views carefully and in print, or privately among specialists before attacking him in public, especially since everyone
speaks highly of Luther's personal life (the deeper importance of
this judgement will emerge in due course). There is a comic side
to Erasmus' struggle with his own nature. Fuming with apprehension, he wrote: 'Theologians in this part of the world are
unpopular at court, and this too they think is my fault. . . .
These men have no confidence in the printed word; their hope of
victory lies entirely in malicious gossip. This I despise, for my
conscience is clear. Their attitude to you has softened somewhat. They are afraid of my pen, knowing their own record; and,
my word, I would paint them in their true colours as they
deserve, did not Christ's teaching and Christ's example point in
quite another direction.' (W 6.392)

Finally, Erasmus wrote more soberly, 'Everywhere we must
take pains to do and say nothing out of arrogance or faction, for I
think the spirit of Christ would have it so. Meanwhile we must
keep our minds above the corruption of anger or hatred, or of
ambition; for it is this that lies in wait for us when our religious
zeal is in full course.' (W 6.393)

Certain of Erasmus' remarks here have lasting importance:
the need for a careful evaluation of Luther's views by a private
discussion among the learned; the importance for his critics of
Luther's reputation for an upright life; the warning to Luther to
avoid discord and faction. While counsels of this sort may seem
almost commonplace, they have a deeper significance, as we
shall hope to demonstrate. In the meantime we shall attempt
briefly to take the two men from this early community of concern to their final debate about free will which captured the
attention of all of Christian Europe.

Erasmus used his influence to try to ensure a fair hearing for
Luther. In October 1519 he wrote from Louvain to Albert, the
cardinal archbishop and margrave of Brandenburg in whose

territories Luther was living. He insisted on Luther's right to be heard. 'It is, I imagine, my Christian duty to support Luther to this extent: if he is innocent, I should be sorry to see him overwhelmed by some villainous faction; if he is wrong, I would rather he were set right than destroyed; for this agrees better with the example Christ has given us, who according to the prophet quenched not the smoking flax and did not break the bruised reed.' (W 7.111)

The fracas around Luther seemed to him a sad distraction from the true task, which was to convert to Christ those who were far from him and to raise the standard of morality among all professing themselves Christian. The source of the evil was the general state of Christian society. 'The world is burdened with ordinances made by man. It is burdened with the opinions and the dogmas of the Schools. It is burdened with the tyranny of the mendicant friars who, though they are servants of the Roman See, have risen to such influence and such numbers that the pope himself—yes, even kings themselves—find them formidable. . . . I do not condemn them all, but there are very many of this description who, for gain and for despotic power, deliberately ensnare the consciences of men. With growing effrontery they now began to leave Christ out of it and preach nothing but their own new and increasingly impudent dogmas. Of indulgences they were speaking in such terms that even the unlettered could not stomach it. This and much like it little by little was sapping the vigour of the gospel teaching; and the result would have been, with things slipping always from bad to worse, that the spark of Christian piety, from which alone the spent fire of charity could be rekindled, finally would be put out.' (W 7.112)

On 15 June 1520 Pope Leo X, pontifical patron of Erasmus' New Testament, composed the Bull *Exsurge Domine* giving Luther sixty days in which to make his submission. Erasmus was dismayed at this further rupture and joined Luther in questioning its authenticity. He tried to prevent the burning of Luther's books, and at the same time urged Froben not to print them. His whole purpose was to extinguish the fires of controversy and work for a more tranquil atmosphere. At this critical moment he did Luther a greater service than Luther ever realized. The youthful emperor Charles V was under consider-able pressure to accept the condemnation of Luther without further consultation of the Imperial Diet. After his coronation at Aachen in November of 1520, the emperor passed through Cologne with his suite, and as an imperial councillor Erasmus was present as was Frederick the Wise, Luther's prince. Frederick sought counsel from Erasmus, who drew up a memo-randum, the *Axiomata*, on how to deal with the affair. These 'axioms' followed the general tenor of Erasmus' views to date, but one in particular should be noted: 'It seems to the advantage of the pope that this affair be settled by the mature deliberation of serious and impartial men; in this way regard will be shown best for the dignity of the pope.' (Ax 143) In collaboration with a friar of whom he approved, a Dominican theologian of Augsburg, named Johann Faber, he devised a proposal for arbi-tration under the august auspices of the emperor with the kings of England and Hungary. Frederick secured from the emperor the promise that Luther would not be condemned unheard. Erasmus returned to the Netherlands.

In the months that followed, Luther's intransigence and refusal to restrain himself in the interests of concord began to take their toll, along with the growing pressure on Erasmus even from sympathetic friends clearly to dissociate himself from Luther. Luther's revolutionary tracts of 1520 had in effect made mediation impossible. Erasmus remained convinced that the real attack was directed against humane letters, and feared for that cause, so precious to his own programme for reform. In February 1521 he wrote from Louvain to Nicolas Bérault, a member of the French humanist circle, 'Luther is piling on both liberal studies and myself a massive load of unpopularity. Every-one knew that the church was burdened with tyranny and cere-monies and laws invented by men for their own profit. Many were already hoping for some remedy and even planning some-thing. . . . Oh, if that man had either left things alone, or made his attempt more cautiously and in moderation! Luther means nothing to me; it is Christ's glory that I have at heart; for I see some people girding themselves for the fray to such a tune that, if they win, there will be nothing left but to write the obituary of gospel teaching.' (W 8.155)

The following May, Erasmus wrote a letter of great importance to Justus Jonas, a humanist graduate of Wittenberg and professor at Erfurt, who had first met him in 1519 as the bearer of Luther's first letter to Erasmus. Erasmus had learned that Jonas was siding with Luther, and his letter was meant not simply for him alone but for a whole circle of German humanists, among them Melanchthon, ready to commit themselves to Luther's cause. Erasmus pleaded that the philosophy of Christ not be sacrificed to national pride and opposition to Rome, however just the provocation. The difference in his outlook from that of Luther is nowhere better illustrated than here.

With full sympathy for the concerns that were tormenting Jonas and his friends, Erasmus recalled his own early hopes of Luther, 'except that at the very first taste of the pamphlets which had begun to appear under Luther's name, I was full of fear that the thing might end in uproar and split the world openly in two. And so I sent warning letters both to Luther himself and to friends of his who might, I thought, carry some weight with him; what advice they gave him I do not know, but at any rate the affair was handled in such a way that there is some danger of remedies wrongly applied making our trouble twice as great.' (W 8.202)

There is further evidence to show Erasmus' unwillingness to see matters of great delicacy and theological weight escape the circle of the initiated, a view at odds with those expressed only five years earlier in the *Paraclesis*. 'When a prudent steward will husband the truth . . . Luther in this torrent of pamphlets has poured it all out at once, making everything public and giving even cobblers a share in what is normally handled by scholars as mysteries reserved for the initiated; and often a sort of immoderate energy has carried him, in my opinion at least, beyond the bounds of justice.' (W 8.203) With a seeming blindness to his own vulnerability to this charge, he went on, 'To give an example, when it would have sufficed to point out to the theologians that they mix in too much Peripatetic, or rather, sophistic philosophy, he calls the whole Aristotelian system the death of the soul.' Confronted by the spectacle of impending schism within his own school of reform, Erasmus now pressed the need for unity and prudence. He was not reluctant to seek scriptural support. 'That spirit of Christ in the Gospels has a wisdom of its

71

own, and its own courtesy and meekness. That is how Christ attuned himself to the feelings of the Jews. He says one thing to the multitudes, who are somewhat thick-witted, and another to his disciples, and even so he has to bear with them for a long time while he gradually brings them to understand the celestial philosophy.' (W 8.203) He appealed to the examples of Peter and Paul, in their slow unfolding of the deeper and more difficult tenets of the Christian mystery, and also to Augustine: 'When he refutes the crazy Donatists, and the Manichaeans who are worse than madmen, his indignation stops short of what the facts deserve, and everywhere there is an endearing admixture of charity as though he thirsted for their salvation, and not their destruction. It was this gentleness in teaching, this prudence in husbanding the word of God that conquered the world and made it pass under the yoke of Christ as no military force, no subtle philosophy, no eloquent rhetoric, no human violence or cunning could ever have done.' (W 8.204)

If Erasmus had not always practised what he was now preaching, he was even-handed in asking Luther and his followers to exercise the same kind of restraint and respect for their opponents as he asked Luther's critics to show towards him. 'And I wonder very much, dear Jonas, what god has stirred up Luther's heart to make him write with such freedom of invective against the Roman pontiff, against all the universities, against philosophy, and against the mendicant orders. Had all he says been true—and those who examine what he has written declare that the case is quite otherwise—once he had challenged so many people, what other outcome was to be expected than what we see now?' (W 8.203) Speaking of his own inadequate acquaintance with Luther's works, and of his 'meagre attainments' to pronounce on such issues, he declared that he could never approve at least Luther's 'method and the way he sets to work. . . . For seeing that truth of itself has a bitter taste for most people, and that it is of itself a subversive thing to uproot what has long been commonly accepted, it would have been wiser to soften a naturally painful subject by the courtesy of one's handling than to pile one cause of hatred on another.' (W 8.203)

In January 1522 a new pope was elected, the same Adrian of Utrecht who, a seeming friend of Erasmus and of his enterprise, had told the University of Louvain to burn Luther's books and force his recantation. He twice invited Erasmus to take up residence in Rome—a compliment of ambiguous allure. The theologians of Louvain began assembling passages in Erasmus' writings which they claimed cast doubt on scriptural authority for religious vows, indulgences, confession, and fasting. Spanish critics of his New Testament living in Rome added their attacks to those of Louvain. In December 1522 Adrian wrote to Erasmus to acknowledge the dedication of his edition of Arnobius the Younger's commentary on the Psalms, and reassured Erasmus as to his confidence in his integrity and scholarship, remarking that the more excellent the learning of scholars, 'the more exposed they must be to the tooth of envy' (W 9.205). Having given this reassurance, however, the pope then asked Erasmus directly to put his learning to the service of the Church in the most pressing issue of the day. 'The affection which we feel for you and the concern we have for your reputation and true glory prompt us to urge you to employ in an attack on these new heresies the literary skill with which a generous providence has endowed you so effectually, for there are many reasons why you ought properly to believe that the task has been reserved by God especially for you.' Erasmus' great intellectual powers, his learning, his readiness in writing 'such as in living memory has fallen to the lot of few or none', his influence and popularity precisely among the Germans where the evil took its rise, such gifts should be used for Christ, who endowed Erasmus with them, for the defence of Holy Church and of the faith. (W 9.205) What is more, this will be the best way to silence those who try to fasten suspicion on him of sharing in Luther's business.

It would have been most difficult for Erasmus to deny Adrian's claims on his talents, and he did not; he temporized and still had not agreed when Adrian died in September 1523. In the meantime Erasmus had been mulling over a work which would not have been a direct challenge to Luther but something much nearer to his method and abilities, a book on peace in the form of a colloquy in three parts between a Lutheran, an opponent, and an arbitrator. The first colloquy would address the question of whether the issues of reform should be tackled in Luther's way; the second discuss his doctrines; and the third would show how the discord could be quieted in such a way that it would not easily start up again. In other words, Erasmus would have given literary reality to an event which had become impossible, a calm, even-handed discussion of the problem of Luther with a prescription for its solution.

The work was never finished, and whatever was written did not survive. Not even his friends encouraged him; he learned that his announcement alone had disappointed and angered all sides, and that by this time no country in Europe was ready for an Erasmian solution. The powerful faculty of theology at Paris was now adding its voice to the attacks of Louvain and the Spanish theologians. A letter, now lost, came from his friend Thomas More in England. What counsel or event persuaded him to change his mind? We do not know, but he began now to sketch out his *Discourse on Free Will*.

The subject was one suggested by Henry VIII, and it had the merit of addressing an issue of deep importance for Erasmus' personal approach to reform. It was also an ancient problem for Christian theology as both Erasmus and Luther knew. In his reply *On the Enslaved Will* Luther thanked Erasmus for going to the heart of their differences instead of debating such comparatively minor issues as purgatory, indulgences, or the nature of papal authority. Erasmus sent an advance copy of his completed text to Henry VIII in March 1524, and it appeared in print in September. It pleased his patrons, but not the theologians. Luther's reply did not appear until December 1525, written with passion and in haste. It proved that Erasmus had chosen his ground well as a rhetorician, since Luther was compelled to defend a view which to the lay reader was by no means appealing. In the words of the distinguished Protestant historian, Gordon Rupp, 'Most of what Luther says and much of the way he says it must set the modern Protestant mind on edge.' (Ru 270–1) Erasmus, on the other hand, defended an attractive position with his familiar grace, courtesy, and clarity. He was the more skilful debater; Luther, the more practised theologian.

The particular issues between then cannot occupy us here, but the debate provides an important opportunity to look more deeply into Erasmus' approach to theological method and to the very nature of the Christian Church itself. Luther was not the only one who was shocked by his seeming indifference to some of the dogmatic issues of Christian tradition, and he was particularly scandalized to find that Erasmus was prepared to declare himself a sceptic in such matters. How could such an attitude be reconciled with any recognizable commitment to the gospel of Christ?

In the course of Erasmus' responses to Luther we have seen his early sympathy and growing concern with Luther's intransigence; we did not find much comment upon Luther's doctrine as such, except that it should be examined carefully by the wise and learned. What Erasmus objected to in Luther with unmistakable clarity from the beginning was his penchant for creating dissension. In his first letter to Luther of May 1519 he warned him against acting in a party spirit, as never pleasing to the spirit of Christ. Shortly after, he told Albert of Brandenburg that he had tried to prevent the publication of Luther's books because he feared the disturbance they would cause. He further stated that he would endure anything personally rather than provoke dissension.

The theme is always prominent, the more so as his fears of Luther grow. 'Tumult', 'sedition'—these are the enemies; at all costs men must strive to preserve peace and concord. By 1526, when Erasmus was ready to break off entirely from any further discussion with Luther, his final bitter accusations are not against his teaching as such, but against his 'arrogant, impudent, seditious temperament' which had brought the whole world into 'ruinous discord'. In fact the willingness of Luther and his followers to disrupt the peace of Christendom means that they are no true reformers.

These objections had been heard from Erasmus before. The charge of creating discord was a significant part of his objection to the scholastics. Their method and immersion in dialectic had brought sectarian division long before Luther appeared on the scene. Writing to Martin Dorp in May 1515, he declared that the prevailing addiction to disputations was deadening and destructive from the very fact that it produced contention and disagreement.

It is clear from this and the general tenor of his writings that concord among Christians was a matter of the utmost gravity to him; in the *Paraclesis* he even suggested that the health of the whole social body depends on it. When this view is compared with the zeal of others, both Catholic and Protestant, for dogmatic truth upon which salvation itself depends, it is easy to see how Erasmus could be dismissed as pusillanimous. Yet he paid dearly for his moderation under furious attack from both sides. There was a deeper issue at stake.

It is discovered in a concept which is almost as recurrent in the thought of Erasmus as *concordia*, and which is closely linked with it—the notion of *consensus fidelium*, the concord or agreement of the faithful. Well before the appearance of Luther, Erasmus had invoked this idea as a reforming principle in relation to the overly complex theology of the day. In his gloss on Matthew 11:28–30 he observed that when Christendom returned at last to the concerns of true piety, theologians and preachers would leave their contentions for their true responsibility of teaching those things which are worthy of Christ, *according to a broad consensus*. With the advent of Luther, divergence from the consensus becomes the ground of Erasmus' objection to his assertions, when he is forced to confront them as such. At the heart of his argument in the *Discourse on Free Will* is Erasmus' declaration that the Holy Spirit would not overlook error in his Church for 1,300 years on a matter which is said by Luther himself to touch the very essence of evangelical teaching.

Immediately after publishing his treatise on the freedom of the will, Erasmus was caught up in a debate in Basle about the nature of the Eucharist. Erasmus insisted that he could not be persuaded by any authority to depart from the 'harmonious agreement of the Christian world'. Two years later, writing on the same matter and refusing once again to dissent from the authority of the Church, he added, 'I call "Church" the consensus of the whole Christian people.' In a subsequent letter to the same recipient, he added to this phrase, 'through the entire circle of the world' (Mc 82).

If we recall his earlier portrait of the Church in the letter to Paul Volz (repeated in the *Ratio verae theologiae* of 1518) we remember his picture of the Christian community as three concentric circles, centred like the rings of a target on the person of

Christ. It was clear there that he saw the Church as a community in which there is an internal, spiritual order; nothing was said of institutional structure. That community originates in baptism, which incorporates individuals into the body of Christ. This is the work of Christ himself through the influence of the Holy Spirit, and the unity of this spiritual body is fundamental to its nature, unity in the work of the Spirit, unity in a common destiny with God.

Since concord is a distinguishing trait of the community duly formed by the action of Christ through the Spirit, the Church as such implies unanimity. In an oft-quoted preface to his 1523 edition of Hilary, Erasmus wrote, 'The essence of our religion is peace and unanimity'—*Summa nostrae religionis pax est et unanimitas*. Consider his paraphrase of John 14: 27 ('Peace I give to you, my peace I leave with you'): 'My peace, which I give to you, reconciles you to God. . . . The peace which I leave with you, binding one to another in mutual concord, renders your fellowship invincible in the face of all adversity.' In another place he wrote, 'The Church is the Christian people, cemented together by the spirit of Christ.' (Mc 84–5)

Unlike Luther, then, Erasmus insisted that Christians do not share in the headship of Christ as individuals; rather, as sharers at the same table, they are made by the Holy Spirit one among themselves. Despite his great belief in lay vocation, he opposed the radical individualism of others in proclaiming the priesthood of all believers. The thought of Erasmus always stressed the corporate identity and responsibility of the community of the Church. God's secret plan for salvation is found only in the solid consensus of the holy Fathers; teaching authority is associated with the ordained hierarchy, which must also however be well-informed about the mind of the faithful. In the *Discourse on Free Will* he reminded Luther that, other things being equal, we can presume that God will more probably communicate his Spirit to those who have been ordained, as one considers it more probable that grace will flow to the baptized rather than the non-baptized. But he saw no guarantee in any institutional form—papal, conciliar, episcopal, or congregational—of absolute authority about the teaching of Christ.

What was the meaning of his insistence on the common mind

77

of Christendom? He held that there could be no dogmatic certainty, including that about justification, without concord. The reason is to be found in his humanistic methodology. In brief, without consensus and concord, its social concomitant, the *logos* could not speak through the Spirit to the community of the baptized. In this ancient, 'true' theology, before the advent of dialectical system, there was no rational organizing principle. The only organizing 'principle' was the text itself. The function of theology was not to produce logical system or formulations to satisfy rational curiosity; it was to penetrate mystery through theological allegory, and to proclaim the mystery in a way that will move God's people to change their lives and the world about them. Thus in Erasmus' method, grammar established the text of revelation where doctrine is discovered, and a grammatical method—that of allegory—also resolves difficulties. Wisdom and understanding accumulate in successive generations through the reflection of the devout and learned. Since the text is the immediate source of divine truth, a learned understanding of biblical languages and texts is fundamental. Necessary too, in the tradition of the classical grammarians, is knowledge of the whole cultural environment of the author, since the grammarian was expected to give general instruction in all of the arts, certainly concerning everything mentioned in the text. And he must know the traditional interpretation held by those closest in time to the moment when the text appeared. At this point Erasmus would invoke the rule in doubtful cases learned from the Fathers themselves: the frail judgement of the individual is supported by the activity of the Holy Spirit working also in the judgement of others, through the *consensus omnium*, the agreement of all.

To Erasmus this ancient method indicated a continuing dialogue of Christ with his flock throughout the ages. Compare Luther's view that 'through the Holy Spirit or the particular gift of God, each man is enlightened so that he can judge in complete certainty in what concerns himself and his own personal salvation, and decide between the doctrines and opinions of all men'. This had been his experience. His personal revelation came in his understanding of Romans 1: 17. In later recollection, Luther described this insight and its bearing on scripture as follows:

'Day and night I tried to meditate upon the significance of these words: 'The righteousness of God is revealed in it, as it is written: the righteous shall live by faith'. Then finally God had mercy on me, and I began to understand that the righteousness of God is that gift of God by which a righteous man lives, namely, faith, and that this sentence—the righteousness of God is revealed in the Gospel—is passive, indicating that the merciful God justifies us by faith, as it is written: "The righteous shall live by faith". Now I felt as though I had been reborn altogether and had entered Paradise. In the same moment the face of the whole of Scripture became apparent to me. My mind ran through the Scriptures, as far as I was able to recollect them, seeking analogies in other phrases, such as the work of God . . . the wisdom of God . . . the strength of God, the salvation of God, the glory of God.' (Mc 94–5) Luther had an organizing principle of his own, a central point from which a totally non-scholastic but nevertheless systematic theology developed. Erasmus, as we have seen, knew no such central point. To him, scripture was an elaborate and mysterious mosaic which, when it was examined with purity of spirit in the light of common understanding and washed clean with the solvents of erudition, revealed to the inward eye of the believer the very face of Christ. If Luther's presuppositions came from his conversion experience, those of Erasmus came from the sapiential traditions of the Patristic exegetes, strongly influenced by a Platonic vision of the intelligible harmony of all creation. For him, belief was always anchored in tradition, but this was not a static order. It developed through time, with the Holy Spirit continually at work fashioning the Church as a community of belief. Through the common agreement of men at once learned and pure of life (hence the importance he attached to Luther's good reputation) we have the only assurance we can have that we are reading correctly the luminous text of the Holy Spirit at work among men, which is the mind of the Church.

In this view of the essentially social character of the activity of the Holy Spirit, Erasmus' difference with Luther is most clear. It is clear also why peace was so important to him. It was essential to preserve the community of discourse by which the Holy Spirit teaches, and was the very sign of truth, deriving from the creative harmony of that society which is the Holy Trinity. Interior peace was advanced as a criterion of spiritual health, and a pre-condition of receptivity to the work of the Spirit.

It is not surprising that Erasmus did not move with Luther. Despite the overlapping of many of their sympathies, Erasmus' whole outlook presupposed a tenacious adherence to the tradition and unity of the community of faith, an adherence which may be labelled 'conservative'. It is a special kind of conservatism, however, since its deepest principle made it impossible for Erasmus simply to judge Luther's doctrines right or wrong. It seems likely indeed, that Erasmus would have looked on Luther's views as he would have looked upon a striking manuscript variant: interesting and possibly significant, but needing the critical reflection of the devout, informed, and learned consensus before its true merit could be appraised.

6 In praise of Folly

In 1521 Erasmus left Louvain for the last time to settle—to the degree that he ever did or could—in Basle, driven from the one place by a rising tide of criticism, drawn to the other by the schedule of publication accumulating at the Froben press. In time, a burgeoning radicalism within the reforming party at Basle would drive him yet again from the haven of the Froben circle, and in 1529 he travelled to Freiburg with his possessions and his faithful housekeeper, Margarete Busslin, to whose patience, common sense, and sturdy independence he undoubtedly owed an unpayable debt. By 1534 a more irenic religious climate prevailed in Basle and the city council adopted a new confession acceptable to Bonifacius Amerbach, Erasmus' younger associate in letters and faithful friend. Amerbach was made rector of the University at Basle in the following May, and he travelled at once to Freiburg to bring back the great man. If a part of his purpose was to secure the prestige of Erasmus for a revival of the university it was all but too late. Erasmus died in July 1536 after a protracted illness. In February he had made Amerbach his heir and the administrator of his estate. This was a sum of five thousand florins invested with the duke of Wurttemburg and the city of Geneva at an interest rate of 5 per cent. This 'foundation', to give it a modern title, became known as the 'Legatum Erasmianum'. The beneficiaries of its earnings were to be the poor, the disabled, the aged, girls in need of dowries, and impecunious students.

Without wishing to make too much of it, this designation of the ordinary people who might be thought of as his personal legatees reminds us forcibly of a side of Erasmus' nature which remains to be dealt with in this brief survey of his vast and varied enterprise, and that is his restless preoccupation with the welfare of the society of his time, especially as that was measured against the professed ideals of those responsible for it. Here he found full scope for satire in his classical idiom, although he was unmistakably indebted to the same degree to

the vivid, robust, and brawling imagery of his medieval prede-
cessors. He was an inveterate moralist, commenting at every
turn on the scene about him, excoriating injustice, delighting in
absurdity, exhorting, extolling, cajoling, teasing, castigating,
lamenting, reviling, and this in his letters, in his annotations, in
almost everything that he wrote, but especially in certain works
that fall under the general heading of *moralia*, his moral writings, which include his great satires.

Among them one important grouping might be termed
'Princes and Peace'. This would include an early rhetorical
address, the *Panegyricus*, written to celebrate the return of
Philip of Burgundy from Spain and printed in 1504. It would
include his chief essay on the duties of the Christian prince, the
Institutio principis Christiani, first published by Froben in
1516, and the *Querela pacis*, the 'Complaint of Peace', published in December of the same year. It would include also certain of the adages from the edition of 1515, an edition that
included all of his most important essays against war: *Scarabeus
aquilam quaerit*, *Aut regem aut fatuum nasci oportet*, *Spartam
nactus es, hanc orna*, *Tributum a mortuo exigere*, and *Dulce
bellum inexpertis*—'War is sweet to those who know nothing of
it'. This last would come to rank as the most famous essay in the
Adages. It was printed separately by Froben in 1517, and was
widely reprinted and translated thereafter, surviving into the
present century as a pacifist classic. Among all the duties before
the Christian prince, that of preserving peace and avoiding war
is the one foremost in Erasmus' mind. It appeared in the
Panegyric of 1504, and it closed the *Institutio*, whose last few
chapters have been translated separately as another peace classic. The *Institutio* was in a tradition familiar in the Middle Ages,
that of the 'Mirror of Princes', designed in this case to instruct
the sixteen-year-old Prince Charles, the future Charles V. It
might well be included therefore among Erasmus' educational
treatises and it stands in sharp contrast to the other contemporary manuals of statecraft, descriptive and analytic in
their approach: Machiavelli's *Prince*, More's *Utopia*, and
Seyssel's *Grant Monarchie de France*. In his programme to form
the perfect, ethical individual for this high office Erasmus drew
most heavily on Plato and Aristotle, stressing in a way charac-

teristic of the humanist outlook the need to direct action toward the 'common good'. In almost no way is it original, therefore, nor did it intend to be, since Erasmus' purpose was, as usual, to pass along the tested moral experience of the past. In one respect, however, it departed from conventional opinion, in denying the theory of the 'just war'. This view, taken over from classical times by Christian authorities like Augustine, rested on an analogy between the administration of justice in the civil state and the rectification of grievances about territorial sovereignty. Erasmus pointed out, however, that there is no such parallel, since it is precisely the lack of an impartial, judicial body to adjudicate differences that brings princes into conflict. The only way to settle such disputes peaceably, therefore, is by arbitration. This idea too, was an ancient one, but it was reinforced by Erasmus with impassioned appeals to all and sundry to apply themselves to the issue of peace among Christians, the necessary condition of all he valued and worked to achieve. The ringing climax of the Complaint of Peace, often quoted, will convey something of his passion:

'I call on you, princes, on whose assent especially the affairs of the world depend, who bear amongst men the image of Christ the Prince: heed the voice of your King, who summons you to peace. . . . I call on you, priests, dedicated to God, to express in all your endeavours what you know is most pleasing to God, and to cut out what is most hateful to him. I call on you, theologians, to preach the gospel of peace and to make your message ring unceasingly in the ears of the people. I call on you, bishops, and you others who are high in the offices of the Church, to see that your authority prevails and peace is held firm in bonds which will last for all time. I call on you, nobles and magistrates, to ensure that your will supports the wisdom of kings and the piety of pontiffs. I call on you all alike who are counted Christians to work together with united hearts. Here you must show how the combined will of the people can prevail against the tyranny of the powerful; here must be the focal point of all endeavour. Eternal concord should unite those whom nature has made one in many things and whom Christ has unified in more, and all should join in a united effort to bring about what concerns the happiness of one and all.' (Q 320–1)

If Erasmus' political writing cannot rank as a work of theoretical originality, its moralistic purpose was precisely the feature that ensured its influence. Among the German principalities, the humanistic concern that secular authority be used to bring about religious reform was particularly well received. It accorded with the established control of local princes over their local Churches. Erasmus' treatise on the *Education of a Christian Prince* bore the authority of his name and propagated an ideal of the Christian magistrate which allowed the next generation of Lutheran reformers to elaborate a doctrine of the State Church.

At the same time it should be noted that Erasmus' ideals, like those of Thomas More, were wholly at odds with the aristocratic traditions of government common to England, France, and most of the German states. This was evident from the very opening lines of the treatise, concerning the birth and upbringing of a Christian prince. 'On board ship we do not give the helm to the one who has the noblest ancestry of the company, the greatest wealth, or the best looks, but to him who is most skilled in steering, most alert, and most reliable. Similarly, a kingdom is best entrusted to someone who is better endowed than the rest with the qualities of a king: namely wisdom, a sense of justice, personal restraint, foresight, and concern for the public well-being.' (I 206) Elsewhere he wrote, 'government depends to a large extent on the consent of the people'. For Erasmus, as we might expect, there was no analogue in kingship to divine sovereignty. For him, as always, the Christian life for prince or peasant was a call to making Christ's example visible and persuasive in the life of the believer. The king who claimed a godlike majesty was imitating a pagan, not the Christian god. That the example of Christ's humility and self-sacrifice was not a plausible ideal for the rulers of his day was a point that came home to him as the years passed, and he would later acknowledge the need for coercive power as the threat of popular violence was borne in upon him. Nevertheless, the earlier, purer ideal was a genuine part of his general doctrine, and if it posed a kind of paradox, he would have much to say about that as well. In this kind of thought, which we have noted before, there is the germ of a profound social and political radicalism, and it was not by chance that Erasmus was taken to heart as a mentor of the radical reformation.

His radicalism in the widest sense is nowhere more evident than in the *Colloquies*, which took their definitive form during the years in Basle. We have alluded to these earlier among his educational works, for that is where they began. In 1518 Froben published a brief collection of conversational exchanges in Latin over Erasmus' name, probably from exercises dictated by him in Paris. Erasmus had not been informed and he was not best pleased; the work was full of faults—but it sold well. He prepared a revised edition which was even more popular. In new editions of 1522 and 1523 the potential offered by these lively introductions to conversational Latin seems to have dawned on Erasmus for the first time, in more developed plots and a broadening horizon of subject-matter. Edition followed edition, each with new dialogues added: ten in 1523, ten more in two editions of 1524, five more in 1526, two in 1527. This went on until nearly the end of his life, the last four editions appearing while he lived in Freiburg. These ebullient, irreverent, dramatic, and rollicking vignettes of common life made their way irresistibly into the schoolrooms of Europe and the imagination of Europeans despite the shock and disapproval of many who saw that, whatever their merits, they were also profoundly subversive. This was not the opinion of conservative theologians alone. Many sympathetic to Erasmus worried about their effect especially on the young; Luther said, on his death-bed, that he would forbid his children to read them.

If we wish to measure the complexity of our subject, consider the context of Erasmus' other activity during these Basle years: editions of the Fathers and of classical authors, new editions of the New Testament, of the *Adagia*, and of his letters; *Paraphrases* on the New Testament, expositions of the Psalms, and new treatises on confession, prayer, the correct pronunciation of Greek, on the Eucharist, on abstinence from meat, on Christian marriage. Above all, there was a ceaseless endeavour to reply to his critics, both Catholic and Lutheran, and, not least, the debate with Luther himself. Amidst such efforts to align himself with those defending the tradition, he continued through the *Colloquies* to present quite another, unmistakably iconoclastic face to his reading public.

Three colloquies appearing first in 1526 may be cited in illustration. 'The Pilgrimage' is one of his most famous essays, recounting his own visits to the shrine of Our Lady at Walsingham, and, in the company of John Colet, to that of St Thomas of Canterbury. At the outset it contains a letter supposedly from the Virgin Mary to Ulrich Zwingli, thanking the reformer for his attack upon her cult which has relieved her from a burden of petitions for quite unsuitable intercessions; 'And sometimes they ask of a Virgin what a modest youth would hardly dare ask of a bawd—things I'm ashamed to put into words.' (C 290) A merchant wishes his kept mistress's chastity protected during his absence, a hired mercenary asks for rich plunder, a gambler offers her a share of his winnings. 'A Fish Diet', an exchange between a fishmonger and a butcher, ranges over a vast canvas but serves to demonstrate the general tendency to turn some disciplinary rules into superstitious beliefs: a nun allows herself to be raped rather than break the rule of silence. 'The Funeral' contrasts the death of two men. The first, a wealthy war-profiteer, is tormented at his death-bed by the greed of his doctors, his parish priest, and a group of friars (all four of the medieval orders being represented) vying to share in his wealth to the complete detriment of his widow and children. The second, a godly man of simple life, dies in tranquillity, having four days earlier attended mass, made a confession, and received the Eucharist. He leaves all he can spare from the necessary provision for his family to the needy, and spends his final hours reading from the scriptures and comforting his family and friends. He receives extreme unction and communion from the parish priest without repeating his confession, dismissing suggestions of a ceremonial funeral and the saying of anniversary masses for the repose of his soul, for 'there is sufficient abundance of merits in Christ, and I have faith that the merits and prayers of the whole Church will benefit me if only I am a true member of it'. This final utterance of the dying man, while as much within the bounds of Catholic orthodoxy as the foregoing, was easily taken for a 'Lutheran' view in the heated atmosphere of the time:

'In two ''briefs'' rests my entire hope. One is the fact that the Lord Jesus, the chief shepherd, took away my sins, nailing them to the Cross. The other, that which he signed and sealed with his own sacred blood, by which he assured us of eternal salvation if we place our whole trust in him. Far be it from me that, equipped with merits and briefs, I should summon my Lord to enter into judgement with his servant, certain as I am that in his sight shall no man living be justified. For my part, I appeal from his justice to his mercy, since it is boundless and inexpressible.' (C 371) If the hand was the hand of Esau, the voice was the voice of Jacob. Or, so many thought.

The *Colloquies* in any case could not be seen alone; they would have recalled forcibly to most of their readers Erasmus' most famous and controversial work, the *Praise of Folly*. The association would be enough to set the teeth of the orthodox reader on edge. The *Folly* appeared first in 1511 in Paris, and in the next year in its authorized edition by Josse Bade. By the time of Erasmus' death there were thirty-six Latin editions, and it had been translated into Czech, French, and German. An Italian version appeared in 1539 and the English translation by Thomas Challoner ten years later. It was received with delight by his immediate circle of friends, including Thomas More and Pope Leo X, but serious criticism also appeared, like that in 1515 from the Louvain theologian, Martin Dorp. Both Erasmus and More replied to Dorp, and from 1515 most editions were accompanied by a commentary by Gerardus Listrius, a learned physician who was rector of a school at Zwolle. Most of his information came from Erasmus. In 1527 the work was condemned by the theologians of Paris and again in 1533. The Sorbonne placed it on a list of condemned books in 1542 and 1543, a list which was the basis for the Index published at Trent in 1564. It was similarly condemned in Milan and Venice, Spain and Portugal, and was included in the works of Erasmus condemned by popes Paul IV, Sixtus V, and Clement VIII. For its life in print it depended upon the presses of England, Switzerland, and the Netherlands.

It began casually enough on a journey to England in the summer of 1509. Erasmus had been tempted to return to England by the death of Henry VII and the prospect of fresh patronage in a place where he had already made friends, people like More and Colet, William Mountjoy, and the archbishop of Canterbury, William Warham. The new king, Henry VIII, was a pupil of

Mountjoy, and Erasmus would have recalled that at an earlier time he had been introduced to the youthful Prince Henry at Eltham by Thomas More. The prospect was enough to persuade him to leave the libraries and cultivated literary associates in the Rome of Leo X, where he may have been offered also a post in the Roman Curia, the gateway to further promotion. In the course of his journey he fell to musing upon a new conceit, a mock encomium in the classical manner in praise of folly—an *encomium Moriae*. It was the very thing to tickle the humanist fancy; the allusion to the name of his English friend and forth-coming host would delight More and all their friends. Para-doxical, ironic, and bantering, with Folly personified as the speaker, it would be a praise of folly by Folly (the genitive being both objective and subjective), and a praise of More, by More under the figure of a licensed fool.

This idea was written down in More's house, by his own account during an illness of a week or so. There is no reason to reject this as a literary device only, if we think of the early pages, where the playful tone is even and consistent. Later it was much rewritten and augmented, like the *Adagia* and the *Colloquies*. It contains in its final versions passages quite inconsistent with the banter of the early section, and the whole is suffused with ambiguity and paradox. From any point of view it was a virtuoso exercise in literary art, by no means perfect, with stretches that invite the reader into a kind of intellectual vertigo.

By Erasmus' own insistence, the work is to be judged as a piece of his evangelical humanism, consistent with the purpose of the *Enchiridion*. This was his contention in his reply to Dorp. 'In the *Enchiridion* I laid down quite simply the pattern of a Christian life. In my book on the education of a prince I openly expound the subjects in which a prince should be brought up. In my *Panegyricus*, though under cover of praising a prince, I pur-sue indirectly the same subject that I pursued openly in the earlier work. And the *Folly* is concerned in a playful spirit with the same subject as the *Enchiridion*. My purpose was guidance and not satire; to help, not to hurt, to show men how to become better and not to stand in their way.' (W 3.114–15) He invokes the authority of Horace: 'To tell truth with a smile, does aught forbid?' What, then, of the unmistakably critical passages? 'I saw how the common throng of mortals was corrupted by the most foolish opinions, and that too in every department of life, and it was easier to pray than to hope for a cure. And so I thought I had found a way to insinuate myself in this fashion into minds which are hard to please, and not only cure them but amuse them too.' (W 3.115)

Erasmus' Lucianesque aims are quite explicit: 'curing' by amusing was his favourite device, inseparable from his most serious scholarship and works of piety in his personal mission to Christian Europe. The *Folly* does not come from the period of his mature thought; even when it was conceived it was only an occasional piece which grew into a fully developed satire, ending unexpectedly with a statement of his religious ideals. Despite its brilliance, it is imperfect in literary form, especially after the original text was altered by sometimes extensive additions, notably in 1514. Nevertheless, it is his best-known work, suffused with an energy which survives even today and in translation, cherished in part because of its very idiosyncrasy. If it does not epitomize his thought, in its elusive stance, captivating wit, impudence, and incisiveness, it seems to lead us more deeply than any other of his creations to the inner recesses of his mental world, to the resources of his demanding, erudite, and mercurial intelligence. For those reasons, although it appears here out of sequence, it will make a fitting conclusion to our survey.

In form the *Folly* is a rhetorical declamation, and it opens with a flourish: 'Folly speaks!' Its captivating, paradoxical tone is apparent from the very beginning—'I'm quite well aware that Folly is in poor repute even amongst the greatest fools . . .', and Folly plunges at once into an expansive account of her indispensable role in making life bearable: 'I am as you see me, the true bestower of good things . . .' (M 87).

Life itself owes its beginning to Folly. 'What man would be willing to offer his neck to the halter of matrimony if he applied the usual practice of the wise man and first weighed up its disadvantages as a way of life? Or what woman would ever agree to take a husband if she knew or thought about the pains and dangers of childbirth and the trouble of bringing up children? So if you owe your existence to wedlock, you owe the fact of wedlock to madness . . .' (M 90).

She warms to her theme: whatever advantages are offered throughout life are provided by Folly. It is not by accident that the happiest, universally enjoyable age of man is the first—that of infants, endowed with the charm of folly by a thoughtful Nature, 'so that they can offer some reward of pleasure to mitigate the hard work of bringing them up'. People on the brink of the grave are likewise recalled to childhood, for compassionate reasons. What is more, devotion to folly even postpones old age; the Hollanders are an example—'for why shouldn't I call them mine? They're my devoted followers, so much so that they've earned a popular epithet (that the older they are, the stupider they become).' Indeed, mother Nature has seen to it that some spice of folly is nowhere lacking, including the gift of woman to man in order to 'sweeten his harsh nature by her folly'. If this draws the wrath of the female sex, after all, this is folly speaking, 'and a woman myself'. The play of paradox intervenes: women are better off than men in many respects: their gift of beauty 'ensures their power to tyrannize over tyrants themselves' (M 95).

The chatter runs on—to parties, to friendship ('winking at your friend's faults, passing over them, turning a blind eye, building up illusions, treating obvious faults as virtues—isn't all that related to folly?'), to marriage ('Goodness me, what divorces or worse than divorces there would be everywhere if the domestic relations of man and wife were not propped up and sustained by the flattery, joking, complaisance, illusions, and deceptions provided by my followers!'), to self-esteem ('since for the most part happiness consists in being willing to be what you are, my Self-love has provided a short-cut to it by ensuring that no one is dissatisfied with his own looks, character, race, position, country, and way of life. And so no Irishman would want to change places with an Italian . . .'), even to great deeds ('no great deed was ever performed without my prompting and no new art discovered unless I was responsible') (M 99). And suddenly a familiar theme emerges. 'Of all deeds which win praise, isn't war the seed and source? But what is more foolish than to embark on a struggle of this kind for some reason or other when it does more harm than good to either side?' From this it is not far to statesmen and philosophers. Remarking that

Plato is always quoted: 'Happy the states where either philosophers are kings or kings are philosophers', Folly observes, 'But if you look at history you'll find that no state has been so plagued by its rulers as when power has fallen into the hands of some dabbler in philosophy or literary addict. The two Catos are sufficient proof of this, I think, when one of them was a disturber of the peace of the republic with his crazy denunciations, and the other showed his wisdom by defending the liberty of the Roman people, and in doing so completely destroyed it.' (M 100)

From this happy beginning, Folly moves on to a sharper focus. Seeing learning and the professions as the discovery of a humanity which had lost the delicious pristine folly of the Golden Age, she turns her bantering discourse to the leaders of Church and State. The most highly valued amongst the learned disciplines are, after all, those 'which come closest to common sense, or rather, to folly'. These are led by medicine ('as it is practised now by so many it is really only one aspect of flattery, just as rhetoric is'), and the law. The philosophers are always laughing at lawyers but the profits of lawyers grow, 'while the theologian who has combed through his bookcases in order to master the whole of divinity nibbles at a dry bean and carries on a non-stop war with bugs and lice' (M 107).

As the declamation proceeds, the irony deepens. Among mortals, those who strive after wisdom are the furthest from happiness, simply because they ignore their humanity and try to adopt the life of the immortal gods. The least unhappy are those who come nearest to the instinctive folly of dumb animals, attempting nothing beyond the capacities of man. Such people have no fear of death; they suffer no pangs of conscience; they feel no shame, fear, ambition, envy, or love. 'Finally, if they come still closer to dumb animals in their lack of reasoning power, the theologians assure us they can't even sin'. (M 109)

Such people are the favourites of kings, and the reason is obvious enough. 'Wise men have nothing but misery to offer their prince; they are confident in their learning and sometimes aren't afraid to speak harsh truths which will grate on his delicate ear.' But the kaleidoscope of argument turns again, since we are next reminded that fools enjoy the peculiar privilege of speaking the truth to the mighty, where the truly wise man has to have two tongues, as Euripides says, 'one to speak the truth with, the other for saying what he thinks fits the occasion. . . . And so for all their good fortune princes seem to me to be particularly unfortunate in having no one to tell them the truth and being obliged to have flatterers for friends.' The fact is that fools can speak truth and be heard with pleasure; 'truth has a genuine power to please if it manages not to give offence, but this is something the gods have granted only to fools' (M 110). The reader is fairly put on notice.

Folly now introduces a theme with a great future in the *Moria* in a seemingly casual defence of her arts against the Stoics, who say that nothing is so pitiable as insanity, and that exceptional folly is near insanity. The place of madness, insanity, folly and its correlatives in human experience will be a recurring issue henceforth. It will allow Erasmus to introduce his surprising climax, and, along the way, to score against some of his favourite targets. Folly moves from gambling, to common superstition, to the superstitious abuse of religion, like indulgences. Scarcely any debased practice of popular religion escapes notice, until Folly despairs of her own catalogue; 'The ordinary life of Christians everywhere abounds in these varieties of silliness, and they are readily permitted and encouraged by priests who are not unaware of the profit to be made thereby. Meanwhile, if some disagreeable wiseacre were to get up and interrupt with a statement of the true facts: "You won't do badly when you die if you've been good in your lifetime. . . . The saint will protect you if you'll try to imitate his life"—if, I repeat your wise man starts blurting out these uncomfortable truths, you can see how he'll soon destroy the world's peace of mind and plunge it into confusion.' (M 115).

The discourse grows more ominous when Folly decides to demonstrate her universal sway, not by enumerating the common types of madness, but by looking at those with a reputation for wisdom: schoolmasters, for example ('by some sort of confidence trick they do remarkably well at persuading foolish mothers and ignorant fathers to accept them at their own valuation'). Grammarians, poets, rhetoricians, writers of books, lawyers ('the most self-satisfied class of people'), along with sophists and dialecticians, quarrelling about 'goat's wool' (an adage), and the philosophers, by which the scholastics are meant. 'Though ignorant even of themselves and sometimes not able to see the ditch or stone lying in their path [a reference to Horace] . . . they still boast that they can see ideas, universals, separate forms, prime matters, quiddities, ecceities, things which are all so insubstantial that I doubt if even Lynceus [an Argonaut whose eyesight could pierce the earth] could perceive them.' (M 126)

This, of course, is only a foretaste of Folly's discourse on the professionals who follow: the theologians, 'a remarkably super-cilious and touchy lot'. None are so unwilling to recognize the services of Folly, yet they are under obligation to her on several accounts, 'notably for their happiness in their self-love, which enables them to dwell in a sort of third heaven, looking down from aloft, almost with pity, on all the rest of mankind as so many cattle crawling on the face of the earth'. The time was at hand for Folly to hold up to ridicule all the futility to which Erasmus had for years objected: the pursuit of theological niceties which owed more, in his view, to the refinements of philosophy than to the sources of Christian faith: 'how the world was created and designed; through what channels the stain of sin filtered down to posterity; by what means, in what measure, and how long Christ was formed in the Virgin's womb; how, in the Eucharist, accidents can subsist without a domicile? . . . What was the moment of divine generation? Are there several filiations in Christ? Is it a possible proposition that God the Father could hate his Son? Could God have taken on the form of a woman, a devil, a donkey, a gourd, or a flintstone? If so, how could a gourd have preached sermons, performed miracles, and been nailed to the cross? And what would Peter have conse-crated if he had consecrated when the body of Christ still hung on the cross?' (M 127)

It is clear by now that Folly's mood and tone changes con-stantly. As the assault on theologians and monks continues, the ways in which they abuse their vocations are contrasted with the religion of the New Testament, especially of Paul, and Fol-ly's voice sounds often enough like that of Erasmus himself. The mask of Folly is always in place, however, teasing and pro-tective. 'Now I think you must see how deeply this section of mankind is in my debt, when their petty ceremonies and silly absurdities and the noise they make in the world enable them to tyrannize over their fellow men, each one a Paul or an Anthony in his own eyes. For my part, I'm only too glad to leave these hypocrites, who are as ungrateful in their attempts to conceal what they owe to me as they're unscrupulous in their disgraceful affectations of piety.' (M 135)

Kings and courtiers are next ('nothing would be so dismal and as much to be shunned as the life they lead if they had even a grain of good sense'), where the issues are luxury, neglect of office, and corruption. Their familiar failings have been adopted by the princes of the Church, who 'think they do well when they're looking after themselves, and responsibility for their sheep they either trust to Christ himself or delegate to their vicars and those they call brothers'. The tone is bitter: 'wherever you turn, to pontiff or prince, judge or official, friend or foe, high or low, you'll find nothing can be achieved without money; and as the wise man despises money, it takes good care to keep out of his way' (M 141).

We are now at the final and most complex section of the *Moria*. Folly announces that, although there is literally no limit to her own praises, every speech must come to an end. First, however, she would like to assure her listeners that there are plenty of great authors who testify to her both in their writings and behaviour. After a brisk reference to some classical sources, Folly turns abruptly to authorities who will carry weight with Christians. For the most part, what follows to the conclusion is a discussion of the Pauline 'fools for Christ's sake'. Folly, with mock modesty, admits that she is venturing into theology ('it oughtn't to be so remarkable if I've acquired something from my long-standing association with the theologians, considering how close it has been'). She now expounds a straightforward account of the folly of the Cross, in which the praise of Christian ecstasy is the climactic theme. The influence of Plato is clear: the myth of the cave is cited directly. Erasmus' sources however are chiefly biblical and patristic. He is quite aware of and rejects any form of Dionysiac possession: his key example is Paul's rapture to the third heaven related in 2 Corinthians 12. M. A. Screech, noting that the myth of the cave was important also to

Ficino, points out that while the realities behind the shadows which delude the ordinary carnal man are, for Erasmus, divine realities, figured in the truths of scripture, for Ficino, this doctrine is closely bound to the hermetic tradition, the 'ancient theology' which was held to antedate the Christian revelation and, to some extent, to supersede it.

It is apparent that Erasmus was strongly attracted (at least at this period of his life) by the Platonic view that the body is a prison house for the soul or mind, but even here he did not venture beyond the bounds of orthodoxy, although he left tempting traces for his critics. He was one with the many humanists both in Italy and in northern Europe who found in Plato the philosophical basis for a doctrine of the immortal soul which was lacking in Aristotle—another stick, incidentally, with which to beat the Aristotelian philosophers and theologians. But on the crucial question of the resurrection of the body Erasmus was unambiguous: it is the basis of Christian hope. When challenged, he also rejected a view found in the tradition of Eckhart and Tauler which his critics accused him of holding: that after death the soul loses its identity, swallowed up or annihilated in God. His main interest, it seems, was with the experience of Christian rapture which was the best clue in this life to the nature of life after death. He was fascinated by Paul's mystical experience, and longed for more information.

At the conclusion of the entire work, Folly explains that the supreme reward of human life is a kind of madness. Plato was on the right track when he wrote (in the *Phaedrus*) that the madness of lovers is the highest form of happiness: 'For anyone who loves intensely lives not in himself but in the object of his love.' An individual in a state of rapture is said to be 'beside himself'; this is a form of madness. When he has returned to his ordinary state, he 'is himself again'. In heaven, Folly continues, 'the spirit will itself be absorbed by the supreme Mind, which is more powerful than its infinite parts. And so when the whole man will be outside himself, and happy for no reason except that he is so outside himself, he will enjoy some ineffable share in the supreme good which draws everything into itself. Although this perfect happiness can only be experienced when the soul has recovered its former body and been granted immortality, since the life of the pious is no more than a contemplation and foreshadowing of that other life, at times they are able to feel some foretaste and savour of the reward to come. It is only the tiniest drop in comparison with the fount of eternal bliss, yet it far exceeds all pleasures of the body, even if all mortal delights were rolled into one, so much does the spiritual surpass the physical, the invisible the visible. This is surely what the prophet [Isaiah, quoted in 1 Corinthians] promises: ''Eye has not seen nor ear heard, nor have there entered into the heart of man the things which God has prepared for those that love him.'' And this is the part of Folly which is not taken away by the transformation of life but is made perfect.' (M 152)

This last is a deliberate allusion to the passage in Luke (10: 42) in which Mary, the contemplative, is praised as having chosen the 'best part' over that of the preoccupied Martha. There follows a description of the state of those experiencing religious ecstasy, 'something which is very like madness'—they speak incoherently, utter senseless sounds, and when they come to, say they do not know where they have been, or remember what they have heard or seen or said or done, 'except in a mist, like a dream'. All they know is that they wish to return to that state when they were happiest, in a bliss that is only the merest taste of the happiness to come.

Suddenly recalling herself, Folly concludes abruptly, apologizing for anything said which seems 'rather impudent or garrulous—you must remember it's Folly and a woman who's been speaking' (M 153). Whereupon appears the final paradox: Folly herself cannot remember what she has said. Are we to understand that what has gone before is to be taken as an image of ecstasy? The enigma is complete.

The foregoing provides only a shadow of the *Moria*, although the general structure and outline is clear enough. A comprehensive reading would have to take into account its classical antecedents, Erasmus' preoccupations at the time, the references to his critics and contemporaries, above all, the fluctuations in rhetorical form, and the richness of classical allusion. It was a work of intellectual virtuosity for the last reason alone.

The enigma remains. The aim of this brief epitome has been to present the leading ideas and concerns of its subject, and perhaps it is clear at least that his was a mind and personality of truly spectacular power, range, and complexity. Excepting only the New Testament, the whole of his vast editorial enterprise has had to be omitted from this account, as has voluminous writing on themes designed to further his enduring enterprise, the regeneration of Christendom. Most of this has by now been absorbed so long into the traditions of European religion and letters as to be invisible, a fate he would no doubt have regarded with satisfaction, although his dismay at the resistance to his most cherished ideals can only be imagined.

We have returned to the early years of this remarkable character with his *Praise of Folly*, whose verve and iconoclastic playfulness are at a far remove from the graver preoccupations of his last years. We are reminded of the slow evolution of his views with the accumulation of learning, the play of event, and, in his private life, the long search for security combined with independence. We know little in detail about his means of existence save that, after leaving the monastery, he lived always by his wits through the gifts of patrons, secular and ecclesiastical, his teaching in universities and in private, the income from ecclesiastical preferments and—least clear of all these—the earnings of his books. These last came not through royalties, the invention of which he did not live to see, but chiefly from the gifts of the influential people to whom he dedicated them.

Through all of his various activities and works the constant tenor of his ideas cannot be doubted, and the philosophy of Christ was always near the focus. In the brief compass of this essay it has been possible only to indicate the foundation of that ideal and some of its principal expressions in their importance for our own moral and intellectual culture. The task of compressing his vast achievement into so small a space inspires an adage for the occasion: 'to fold a featherbed into a matchbox'. Inevitably the effort bestows a heightened consistency on Erasmus' writings as the desire to present them sympathetically may confer an air of partiality which is unintended. A full account would run far beyond our prescribed limits, but it would expose, *inter alia*, a personality quite unlike the ideal Erasmus painted of the faithful Christian inspired solely by habits of charity and irenicism. The illegitimate orphan had little insulation on his nerve ends, and he flew sometimes even at the mildest of his critics with a pen that could stab and bite. He was charged by some, and not without reason, with vindictiveness, ingratitude, and duplicity. It is tempting to think that his preoccupation with the disparity between Christian ideals and the daily conduct of those who profess them was rooted in a deep awareness of his own shortcomings.

Despite those he dominated his age through the sheer intellectual impact of his achievement combined with his wide-ranging evangelical concern. The whole was animated by his personal fervour, wit, and brilliant, insinuating style. He did not possess the most innovative mind of his generation; to look no farther than the immediate circle of northern colleagues, Vives, for example, was capable of more daring insight in his programme for the education of women and the care of the poor. No one, however, could approach the scale of Erasmus' personal contribution to the restoration of the sources of European learning and religion, nor rival his sweeping vision of a Christendom renewed by the propagation of a reformed educational programme and the elevation of the lay estate, this being the final consequence of Erasmus' insistence on the equal sanctity of vocations among the baptized.

His scepticism toward theological speculation—he declared that it was more pious to adore the unknown than to debate the unknowable—with his assaults on common pieties that seemed to him to distract from the proper focus of devotion, his insistence that most differences between Christians were of no final consequence and should be treated with mutual tolerance and respect—this attitude of mind, proclaimed in his restless outpouring of letters, satires, educational and devotional treatises, scholarly annotations and controversies, meant that even without the Lutheran convulsion, the Christian world could never have looked the same again. In the midst of all of this, however, he insisted that his sole aim was peace and spiritual unity, and that the tradition should be respected always; perhaps his scepticism about the attainment of final dogmatic truth in itself ensured that. Above all, he declared, those professing to be Christians should bend their every energy to live well.

To help toward that goal he assembled a programme that secured the pattern of liberal education for four hundred years. Whatever the ideal might become in the hands of generations of schoolmasters, it began with his belief in the power of wisdom, the tested moral experience of the race, to inform and renew our life together. Such wisdom, the generation of the Word, could be attained only with unremitting labour to comprehend the foundational texts, sacred and profane. To that task he brought unsurpassed industry and acumen. He forever raised the stakes of scholarship, and his personal skill was such that later generations, more practised in the science of philology, would pause before the sheer range of his erudition and his almost unerring instinct for a false attribution or forgery.

Never again would anyone be able to combine such learning with such unceasing devotion to the issues of the day. His correspondence is the best index of the daily activity of one who has come ironically to symbolize the withdrawn scholar. In his correspondence as in his printed works, he created a commonwealth of learning with access to the most influential persons, lay and ecclesiastical, in almost every corner of Europe.

In his own lifetime all of this seemed to come to nothing, and his final days were haunted by the seeming collapse of his cherished project for the peaceful renewal of a world of civility and understanding. Yet it left a legacy of common loyalties and ideals perhaps more durable than he dreamed, and wherever the cause of international peace and concord is admired, the name of Erasmus is still invoked.

Beyond all of this a unique voice remains, best discovered, no doubt, in the *Folly*. In the voice there lives on still the virtuoso personality and critical intelligence, audacious, paradoxical, elusive yet captivating, intimate yet forever alone. The motto of his personal seal was *Cedo nulli*—'I yield to no one.' The speaker was Death. It was also Erasmus.

Suggestions for further reading

The extensive modern literature on Erasmus is best approached through the bibliography of Jean-Claude Margolin, dealing in successive volumes with publications since 1936. These are: *Quatorze années de bibliographie érasmienne, 1936–1949* (Paris, 1969), *Douze années . . . 1950–1961* (Paris, 1963), and *Neuf années . . . 1962–1970* (Paris, 1977). Further volumes are promised.

Until recent years, the standard edition of Erasmus' letters and works was the folio *Opera omnia* published in Leiden in 1703–6 and known in the literature as LB. The critical edition of the correspondence is that by P. S. Allen, the *Opus epistolarum* in 11 volumes with an index volume added (Oxford, 1906–47). A new, critical edition of the works published in Amsterdam and known as ASD is sponsored by the Royal Dutch Academy and the International Union of Academies, and began to appear in 1969. A comprehensive English translation of Allen's edition of the correspondence (updated with respect to both texts and annotations) and of an extensive range of the works (excluding only Erasmus' editions and translations from the Greek) is being published at the same time by University of Toronto Press as *The Collected Works of Erasmus* (1974–   ). Of this series, known as CWE, 9 volumes of correspondence (to 1523) and 12 volumes of works have appeared to date. All of the citations in this book are taken from the relevant volumes of CWE with the exception of two. The *Paraclesis* is taken from the convenient, one-volume collection by John C. Olin, *Christian Humanism and the Reformation* (New York, 1987). The colloquies are quoted from the translation by Craig R. Thompson published in one volume in Chicago in 1965. This has been revised and Thompson's complete edition will appear soon in two volumes with full annotation in the CWE series. In addition, Toronto has published a three-volume biographical register of the correspondents of Erasmus and others mentioned in his works and letters, as *Contemporaries of Erasmus* (1985–7). The text of the *Praise of Folly* which appears in CWE is translated by Betty Radice, and appeared originally in Penguin Classics in 1971. The annotator of that translation, A.H.T. Levi, is editor of the volume (27) of CWE in which the *Praise of Folly* appears along with other of Erasmus' satires. His introduction will be useful in understanding the implication of the term 'satire'.

Among modern biographies those by Johan Huizinga, *Erasmus and the Age of Reformation* (New York, 1924) and Roland H. Bainton, *Erasmus of Christendom* (New York, 1969) are still available. The most recent biography, that by Cornelis Augustijn, has appeared in Dutch and German, and will be published shortly in English in Toronto. A favourite account of Erasmus' life and times remains that of Margaret Mann Phillips, *Erasmus and the Northern Renaissance*, first published in London in 1949, and revised and reissued after several reprintings in 1981.

With respect to individual works, Mrs Phillips was the author also of the most important monograph to be written to date on the subject of the *Adagia*: *The 'Adages' of Erasmus* (Cambridge, 1964). On the colloquies, apart from the work of Craig Thompson, the monograph of Pierre Bierlaire should be noted: *Les Colloques d'Erasme* (Paris, 1978). On the controversy with Luther, Ernest F. Winter translated and published an edited version of the debate as *Erasmus–Luther: Discourse on Free Will* (New York, 1961). A helpful discussion referred to in the text is that of Gordon Rupp, 'Luther and Erasmus, 1525' in a collection of his studies on Luther, *The Righteousness of God* (London, 1953). Also of interest on the theological debate is Harry J. McSorley, *Luther Right or Wrong?* (New York, 1968). Recent accounts of the place of humanism in the establishment of the Reformation are those of James M. Estes, *Christian Magistrate and State Church: the Reforming Career of Johannes Brenz* (Toronto, 1982), and of James M. Kittelson, *Wolfgang Capito: from Humanist to Reformer* (Leiden, 1975). On the topic of Erasmus' political views, see James D. Tracy, *The Politics of Erasmus* (Toronto, 1978).

The most important single work dealing with the intellectual formation of Erasmus is the recent two-volume study of Jacques Chomarat, *Grammaire et rhétorique chez Erasme* (Paris, 1981).

M. O'Rourke Boyle, *Erasmus on Language and Method in Theology* (Toronto, 1977) is valuable. Some collections also contain suggestive essays on these and other themes, notably: J. Coppens, *Scrinium Erasmianum* (2 vols., Leiden, 1969); *Colloquium Erasmianum*, Actes du colloque international réuni à Mons (Mons, 1968); J.-C. Margolin, *Colloquia Erasmiana Turonensia* (2 vols., Paris, 1972). The second volume of the Coppens collection contains the essay by James McConica, 'Erasmus and the Grammar of Consent', which is cited in the text.

On the New Testament scholarship of Erasmus see, in particular, Erika Rummel, *Erasmus' Annotations on the New Testament* (Toronto, 1986), and Albert Rabil, Jr., *Erasmus and the New Testament* (San Antonio, 1972). A facsimile edition of Erasmus' annotations on the Gospels by Anne Screech appeared in London in 1986, with an introduction by M. A. Screech. The important article by Andrew Brown referred to in the text is 'The date of Erasmus' Latin translations of the New Testament', in *Transactions of the Cambridge Bibliographical Society*, vol. 8, pt. 4, '1984' (1985).

The literature on the *Praise of Folly* is immense. An important recent account of one aspect of the work is that by M. A. Screech, *Ecstasy and the Praise of Folly* (London, 1980). Further helpful information can be gathered from the introduction and annotations of A. H. T. Levi to the Penguin Classics edition mentioned above.

Index

Index

Dordrecht, 5
Dorp, Martin, 75, 87, 88

Eckhart, Meister, 95
Eltham Palace, 88
Elzevir Greek Testament, 44
Epicurus, 47
Erasmus:
    ancient wisdom and, 15–17, 23, 53
    birth and family, 4–5, 7
    Cambridge, lectures at, 39
    Colet and, 31–4
    dispensations sought by, 4
    editorial procedures of, 34–5
    educational masters, 14–15
    goes to Italy, 39
    homeland of, 1, 99
    interest of, today, 2–3
    'Legatum Erasmianum', 81
    Luther, debate with, 66–80
    memory, personal, 14
    memory systems and, 21–2
    ordained priest, 18
    pagan learning and, 7, 8, 9–17, 45,
        52, 53, 61
    'philosophy of Christ', 45–62, 97
    private tutor at Paris, 19
    proverbs, role of, 20, 25
    schooling of, 5–8
    stay at Oxford, 31–4
    university of Paris and, 18
Erasmus, works of:
    Adagia, 10, 13, 23–9, 30, 31, 39, 40,
        45, 54, 66, 82, 85, 88
    Adagiorum collectanea, 24, 25, 31,
        34
    Annotations on the New Testament,
        30–1, 40–1, 42, 43, 44
    Antibarbari, 9–17, 18, 31, 45
    Arnobius the younger, edition of, 73
    Axiomata, 70
    Colloquia, 19, 63, 64, 85–7, 88
    Compendium vitae, 4–5
    De conscribendis epistolis, 19, 39
    De copia, 19, 22, 39
    De libero arbitrio (On Free Will), 74,
        76–7
    De ratione studii, 19, 20–3
    Ecclesiastes, 65
    Enchiridion, 36–7, 38, 49–62, 66,
        88; translations of, 49;
        anthropology of, 55–7; rules, 58–9;

Christian vocation in, 60–1;
        portrait of the Church in, 61–2
Hilary, edition of, 77
Institutio principis Christiani, 82,
    84
Jerome, edition of letters of, 14,
    33–6, 38, 40, 65, 66
John Chrysostom, translation of, 39
Latin version of New Testament,
    30, 38, 41
Leiden edition of works, 2
'Letter to Grunnius', 8
New Testament, edition of, 10, 14,
    29, 30–44, 45, 49, 64, 66, 85, 93,
    97; manuscripts used in printing
    of, 42; Spanish critics of, 73–4;
    see also Latin version of,
    Annotations on
Opus epistolarum, 1529, 8
Panegyricus, 82, 88
Paraclesis, 45–9, 66, 71, 76
Parallels (Parabolae), 40
Paraphrases on the New Testament,
    85
Paul, commentary on epistles of, 43
Plutarch, translations from, 40
Praise of Folly (Moriae encomium),
    27, 29, 30, 39, 59, 66, 87–99;
    condemnations of, 87
Psalms, expositions on the, 85
Querela pacis, 82, 83
Ratio verae theologiae, 61, 76
St Basil's commentary on Isaiah,
    translation of, 39
satires of, 82
Spongia, 6
Valla's Collatio novi testamenti,
    edition of, 38
Valla's Elegantiae, epitome of, 19,
    33
Erfurt, university of, 71
Estienne, Robert, Greek Testament of,
    44
Euripides, 21, 39, 92

Faber, Johann, 70
Fell, John, 43
Ficino, Marsilio, 55, 95
Fisher, John, bishop of Rochester, 19,
    39
Fisher, Robert, 19, 23
Florence, 31

104

Index